U R TITANIUM

GINNY W. FRINGS, Ph.D.

Copyright © 2017 Ginny W. Frings, Ph.D.

All rights reserved. No part of this book may be used or reproduced by any means, graphic, electronic, or mechanical, including photocopying, recording, taping or by any information storage retrieval system without the written permission of the author except in the case of brief quotations embodied in critical articles and reviews.

Scripture taken from the NEW AMERICAN STANDARD BIBLE ®, Copyright © 1960, 1962, 1963, 1968, 1971, 1972, 1973, 1975, 1977, 1995 by The Lockman Foundation. Used by permission. (www.Lockman.org)

WestBow Press books may be ordered through booksellers or by contacting:

WestBow Press
A Division of Thomas Nelson & Zondervan
1663 Liberty Drive
Bloomington, IN 47403
www.westbowpress.com
1 (866) 928-1240

Because of the dynamic nature of the Internet, any web addresses or links contained in this book may have changed since publication and may no longer be valid. The views expressed in this work are solely those of the author and do not necessarily reflect the views of the publisher, and the publisher hereby disclaims any responsibility for them.

Any people depicted in stock imagery provided by Thinkstock are models, and such images are being used for illustrative purposes only. Certain stock imagery © Thinkstock.

ISBN: 978-1-5127-8501-2 (sc)
ISBN: 978-1-5127-8503-6 (hc)
ISBN: 978-1-5127-8502-9 (e)

Library of Congress Control Number: 2017906755

Print information available on the last page.

WestBow Press rev. date: 08/25/2017

Dedication

To Michael, Eric, Faith, and Kristen… who recognize the power of both the spoken and the written word.

Acknowledgements

Father, Son, Holy Spirit – thank you for your effervescent presence and spiritual presents... You lift me up beyond myself and closer to You.

Michael Frings – thank you for sharing this adventuresome life journey together... for being strong...and for loving me.

Eric, Faith, and Kristen Frings – thank you for being the most awesome children... Mama loves you.

Albert Cloudy – Ok, so you are the poet extraordinaire, Mr. Cloudy... thank you for sharing your gift of words woven together with meaningful messages. You are a blessing in the lives of all who know you.

Shelly Justin – where do I begin? You brought poetry into Albert's life... you are a beautiful gifted teacher and poet who inspires others to flourish in their own gifts... thank you, my friend.

Matt Kochera – Ok now... you, dude, inspired me to get serious with fitness... taught me how to focus on the lift... and how to get past my own perceived limitations. I know... right? You challenge me to reach for the next level of fitness. Look forward to more Team M.O.V.E. workouts and film shoots. Come on... Let's do this...

Eileen Martin – Wow girlfriend... love you so much... our friendship began at Sheltering Arms and has grown so beautifully through the years. Thank you for always inspiring me to trust God and grow stronger… you are truly a blessing in the lives of this Frings family.

Tony Green - thank you for your friendship, insights, and challenging me to write a spirit-filled proclamation from fear. Pretty cool how God continues to cross our life paths…

Amber Smith – so awesome to know you… all beginning with our daughters' friendship… your beautifully inspiring artwork graces the cover of this book… and your loving presence in my life and in the lives of so many help us all to weave a fabric of caring and love reaching into the friendships and relationships within our lives… thank you for sharing your gifts.

Lauren Drummond – Sooooo… it's no coincidence that our paths crossed five years ago during our children's swimming lessons… and then crossed so many times since… to now developing a new media series focusing on relationship reconciliation and reparation for so many communities in need of this initiative right now… God is the Director… we are the actors… it's both an honor and a pleasure to be co-starring with you my friend… love you sister in Christ.

Bernie Aniciete – Now, dude… you are the truly gifted videographer who brought M.O.V.E. to life! To work with me and Matt… that's a challenge within itself… the outtakes alone could fill a hard drive… thank you for your insightful direction and patience… We are so excited to work with you… and the next book trailer and movie pitch look to be interesting experiences.

Janice Wenger – thank you for always being a light in my life… our daughters' friendship has been the catalyst for so many wonderful family gatherings. You, Janice, inspire so many of us who cross your life path… keep doing what you are doing… love you, girlfriend.

Sandy Golden, CEO, Concerned Angels, Inc. – Alright now… Captain Sandy and Malibu Barbie are on a mission from God to help save lives… cool to be re-inventing Concerned Angels after all these years… truly a calling… look forward to the journey with you and Marianne… you two are blessings in my life and in the lives of so many.

Christine Schmidt – Ok… so God crosses our paths in interesting ways… we purchased your previous residence in St. Louis… we are both Christian inspirational authors… and you my dear share your story within the pages of this book… thank you for following God's leadings… am blessed to know you, Christine.

Christa O'hearne – You, my friend, light up my life every time we connect… I know… right… we are next door neighbors and often on the go with family activities… I always look forward to spending time with you… you are an inspiration… love you every day.

Jack Smith – thank you, Jack, for your inspiring presence and encouraging words… you welcomed me and my family to Xavier University when I didn't even know where to park… and then you encouraged me through every day of my four years there as faculty… your smile… your words of wisdom… you're a gift to all of us who know you.

Regan Stevens Branch – you, my niece, are an inspiration to so many lives… including mine… your strength and drive to achieve your goals encourage me to go for the next step on this life adventure leading to a deeper relationship with Jesus Christ… building muscle in the gym and honing spiritual growth in the sanctuary… thank you for recognizing God's presence each day of your life and your willingness to share your experiences with the rest of us. Love you girlfriend.

Kim Vetter – alright, you realize that our meeting at The Crossing explorations class was not just a coincidence… God has woven our life paths together for a reason… His purpose… am so excited to journey with you into the next destination with Jesus leading the way… in the spiritual… intellectual… and physical gyms. Come on… let's do this… time to focus on the next lift.

Judy West – thank you for the numerous conversations about spiritual gifts… recognizing the gift of apostleship… your sense of humor and God's direction to be shared into our lives… blessed to know you.

Bill Jiranek – Ok… so since my car wreck…and 12 surgeries in 6 years… 3 of those surgical experiences were successfully completed by you. Now, later… we have the opportunity to collaborate on a research project designed to make a difference in many lives… thank you. Let's do this.

Chris Foeldi – So blessed to connect with you in God-directed conversations about His grace and leadings in our lives… books… movies… Bible studies… C2C to come… consultant or co-author… ?

Monica Orban – Love you girlfriend… oh how the miles of walks and talks with you during the past five years have helped to shape me… physically, mentally, and spiritually… thanks for being my friend, Veronica…always Betty.

Cover artist

Amber Smith is a writer, artist, and small business owner. She is a fan of vibrant colors, tall shoes, meaningful conversations and lyrics, red wine, coffee, and all things beach. She lives in Chesterfield, Missouri with her husband, children, and many pets.

coffeebecomesher.org
a2zselfiecompany.com

Poet: Albert Cloudy

I'm from the inner city of Saint Louis. I started out in public schools till first grade when I came to Rockwood (my second home) from first till twelfth. I became a venturing out person. I was in afjrotc, musicals, plays, poetry slams. And, I joined track. When I had time, I would do more. I have been through a lot in those 12 years that made me who I am today, from the city life to the county life. I found out that words go a long way! Now, I'm a massage therapist and I still have a way with the words.

Table of Contents

Prologue		xv
1	*T*rust	1
2	*I*ncentives	16
3	*T*ime	34
4	*A*rmor	49
5	*N*ext... Step	75
6	*I*nvitation	89
7	*U*nderstanding	115
8	*M*eaning	134
Take-Away		157
Notes		159

Prologue

"The first step is you have to say that you can." Will Smith

"Time to stand up and take the first step," Mark says. Ginny responds, "I can't." She looks down at her two atrophied legs, sitting lifeless in the wheelchair. At this point, she has no idea how to make them move at all. Since the car wreck, she has had no function of her legs or left arm. Now, months later, the doctors say that she has healed enough to try standing. Mark kneels down to look her in the eye. He says, "Come on, Ginny. I'm here to help you." "I'm gonna fall," she says. He replies, "I won't let you fall," as he reaches to place the harness strap around her waist…

***

The above dialogue is real. Recalling this conversation still brings tears to my eyes as I remember the intensity of my fears at that moment in time… the fear of falling… the fear of the unknown… fearful of the pain that I was about to experience. I was thinking, *Will I be able to stand at all? Will I ever walk, again? I can't even remember how to walk. It will hurt when I fall. I just can't do this. Not today.*

Here and Now…
So, why is this book titled *U R Titanium*? Well, first of all, when you see the word "titanium," what image comes to mind? Military planes… sports equipment… automobiles… others? For some of us, we think of joint prostheses… knees… hips… that sort of thing. Titanium images

suggest grand strength without the heavy physical weight of a metal. Here's an interesting fact: solid titanium has a melting point of 3024 degrees Fahrenheit and a boiling point of 5949 degrees Fahrenheit.[1] In other words, this strong and lightweight metal can "stand the cold" and "take the heat." The famous Blackbird SR-71 fighter jet is primarily Titanium – able to survive extreme velocities of Mach 3.5+ and altitudes of 80,000 feet.[2]

So, we can say that titanium represents strength during times of extreme circumstances. This point could indicate why we now see products such as titanium golf clubs, tennis racquets, balls, even names of cars… apparently the idea that something has the properties of titanium is appealing to consumers. And, I agree. Having my deteriorated right hip replaced with a titanium total hip joint enables me to walk and water ski without pain… except of course when I wipe out…lol.

As the saying goes… No pain no gain… seriously?
Everyone deals with pain at some point in their lives… whether it is physical… emotional… relational… or spiritual. And, with pain often comes fear - fear that the pain could worsen… fear that the pain will never be cured… resolved… or healed. That said, let's try to tease out the answer to this question: To whom or what do we look for strength and endurance when we are trying to deal with life's struggles, i.e., life's aches and pains? Or, let me ask you this: Is it the struggle itself which makes you want to be stronger? Sometimes, when we are trying to work through challenges, fear overtakes us and it feels as if we are being burnt… or maybe refined… by the fires that are blazing in our life path. In this book, we will walk through those "fires" together and come out on the other side stronger, more resilient, and with hope.

More is better… really?
So, what about the constant need to get our "stuff" upsized and quicker? Doesn't it feel as though we are trying to fly through life - higher and faster? We are setting ourselves up to crash and burn, so to speak, unless we learn how to let God work within us to fearlessly reach the speeds,

heights, and destinations which He envisions on the flight path He has mapped out for each of us. We will call this process of "letting go and letting God build us up" a *Titanium Transformation*.

Titanium Transformation…
So, most of you have probably heard the phrase, "There's strength in numbers." Yes? Meaning that we need not attack our problems alone… we need an army to walk with us through the trials and tribulations of everyday life. It takes a village… oh no… sorry to be so cliché… but let's face it… we need friends. Period. Ok, now we are going to talk about the "relationship" word… yes… we need to learn how to develop relationships which will help us to become stronger. In the pages of this book, we will learn more about developing stronger relationships – both horizontally with people and vertically with our God.

God says, "Do not fear, for I am with you;" (Isaiah 43:5) He provides us with the strength to persevere while knowing He is there beside us. The thing is that so many times in life we forget to pray, that is, to ask Him to carry us when we do not see the opportunities which He has planned for us… ways in which He will direct our decisions. And, we forget to trust God. Let's take that first step - closer to God.

Mirror, mirror…
For those of us who have physical scars and for those of us who have emotional scars, what do we see when we look in the mirror? In my previous book, *Navigate with God*, we learned about "scars being reminders of perseverance rather than blemishes of tragedy." [3] God carries us through our experiences if we will let Him. He is in us and all around us. Is His light shining through you? And, back at you when you look in the mirror? In personal fitness training, we learn to direct our attention to the image in the mirror, rather than the numbers on the scale. What does your reflection say about you? Are you showing God's light and love to others? That question was resonating in my mind while driving home from the gym one evening. Then, David Guetta's song, "I am Titanium,"[4] came on and the words stuck with me… partly because

I am literally made of titanium… remember the hip… the metal arm… the leg. But, as I listened to the song, I started to realize that his lyrics could be used to address the emotional and physical tragedies of being bullied, judged, and ridiculed. We are all different. Every human being possesses both strengths and weaknesses. How do we help edify each other's strengths and work together to mitigate the weaknesses? Remember, God reminds us that when we are weak, He is strong. He places people in each other's paths as a way to connect the members of the Body of Christ to make our lives more fruitful and this world more unified. The band, Nickelback, sings the song, "If Everyone Cared…"[5] and Casting Crowns sings about all of us actually acting upon our calling to be members of the Body of Christ in "If We Are The Body."[6] We are His healing hands… His encouraging voice… His strong feet… His understanding heart. We will explore this idea.

Let's talk…
In today's high-tech world, communication of ideas and thoughts can be instantaneous. Oftentimes, we speak, i.e., text, before we think about the consequences of our words. And, when on the receiving end of hurtful dialogue, we do not always know how to respond. We've all heard, and probably said at times, the phrase: "Sticks and stones may break my bones, but words will never hurt me." Actually, words can hurt. They can even have fatal consequences. I know it can be hard to stand when you are being verbally abused. It's like people are trying to tear you down. So, let's focus on some physical and emotional strength training to build you up. Ok, then - it's time to hit the spiritual gym. Let's go. We can do this together.

Let's begin by trusting God to help us F.O.C.U.S. on the lift…
In this book, you will experience *Focus on the Lift* exercises within each chapter. These activities will help you learn how to draw strength and mitigate fear as you begin your own *Titanium Transformation*. Here are some thoughts to contemplate as you ready yourself to begin this Transformation into a stronger you. First, let's define a few terms so

that we are all on the same page… no pun intended. In each exercise, we will need to remember to F.O.C.U.S. where:

F is Flow – Allow God's strength and grace to flow into and through you. As you continue to "work out" the lessons in each chapter, you will feel yourself becoming stronger and with a strengthened sense of spiritual renewal.

O is Others – We operate every day within a cloud of witnesses – others to whom we are being called to witness and lead to Christ. Let's learn to act and react in a manner which lifts up people around us.

C is Cues – Ask God to increase your awareness of His indicators – signals of His presence – whether He is affirming your actions or alerting you to a different course of action. Physical trainers are always watching the faces of their clients, checking for any signs of distress or questions. Look for the cues.

U is Undone – To progress toward your next goal, you must step outside your comfort zone and do your best to take each rep to fail – adding resistance – doing negatives – and adding progressive overload to build.

S is Super set – In the gym, we can super set different exercises when working particular muscle groups - meaning no breaks between sets of reps within a circuit training routine. In life, we can build stamina and momentum in much the same way as we move between tasks during the day… keeping our minds active, increasing awareness, and learning how to draw energy from our activities instead of feeling the depletion of our personal energy reserves. This process takes time to develop.

Upon completing the *Focus on the Lift* exercises within the pages of this book, you will begin to F.O.C.U.S. on each task, and naturally start to recognize the building facets in your life, so as to draw God into your strengthening routines each day.

Now, let's clear our minds and focus on the words of this young poet named Albert Cloudy.

STRENGTH
by Albert Cloudy

In life there becomes a time
Opportunities and hardships will come swarming in
You become more engaged and less pretend
You'll need all the power you have called strength
When the overwhelming feeling reels you in
It requires you to be strong
To let nothing or no one pull you along
Grasp and hold on, don't let go
The strength and power to not give in
Physically and mentally tough, to the point which others can't comprehend
God doesn't place anything in front of you that you can't overcome
But to push through it so you can see what you become.

©2016 Albert Cloudy. All rights reserved. Used with permission.

In *U R Titanium*, we will learn ways to build the strength and relationships we need to thrive in the midst of unwarranted criticism and ostracism. We will explore our roles as members of the body of Christ. We will accept God's "invitation to high tea" and see how a "string of pearls" can be an accessory to a "coat of armor." We will "dance in the rain" and learn that there is always time for a "high five" on the path to serenity.

Chapter 1

∞∞∞∞∞ Trust ∞∞∞∞∞

Trust in the Lord with all your heart
And do not lean on your own understanding.
In all your ways acknowledge Him,
And He will make your paths straight. (Proverbs 3:5-6)

Following God's lead…
Jesus knew of His life's prophecy. And, He knew that the Pharisees were watching Him very closely seeking to find fault in His ways so that they could convict Him. But, Jesus trusted and continued to follow His Father's directions to walk the path of life that lay before Him. In Luke 6, we read a story about Jesus' interactions with the Pharisees, His healing touch, and prayerful selection of His twelve disciples – all the time knowing that His days here on earth were numbered. He walked the path less traveled, guided by His Father's hand. And, He knew someone close would one day betray Him with an end game of death on a cross. Jesus exemplifies unconditional faith, dedication, and trust in His Father. Do each of us show that level of trust in God? That's something to think and pray about…

Now, here is Albert Cloudy's poetic insight into the idea of placing your trust in someone.

Ginny W. Frings, Ph.D.

TRUST
by Albert Cloudy

Have the ability to give over a part of you
It's not easy to be gained nor kept
Confident in yourself and the other
To look straight in their eyes
Take a part of you and say "I trust you!"
Knowing deep down that you are sure
That the path you're going down
Could be taking advantage of
Which is not needed but someone to rely on
To come to in extreme circumstances
Tell the biggest secret you ever told
And rely on with whatever you come with
Remember you have the ability to give it mutual to keep it
Because you can't make it without it
There's nothing more stronger to have than trust.

©2016 Albert Cloudy. All rights reserved. Used with permission.

Hey… can I trust you?
"Can I trust you?" How many times in our lives have we asked that question of a friend or relative right before sharing an innermost thought? And, not to stir up bad memories… but oftentimes… at least in my experiences… those deepest thoughts shared with one person became known by many. We all feel somewhat vulnerable when another person betrays our confidence. When it's our own private "stuff" that we just need to share with someone, how do we learn with whom we can talk openly? Can trust be earned? Can trust be renewed?

As a university professor, I have designed and taught many business courses where upon studying pertinent real-life ethics cases, we always concluded that business professionals should carry an attitude of what I term "Professional Skepticism" when analyzing deals and learning with whom they can honestly conduct business transactions, i.e., trust. There, we are talking about horizontal interactions between people. Every day, we all experience horizontal interactions when we communicate with other people, but what about vertical interactions between ourselves and God? Within the spiritual realm, we are called to trust God, like in Proverbs 3:5-6 and Psalm 27, for examples. And, Psalm 91 instructs us not to worry. IPeter 5:7 tells us to cast all our cares on the Lord. Will worrying add a minute to your life? No. Fretting over experiences for which you have no control can actually hinder the quality and quantity of your time here. Bottom line: God's got our back, even when we feel like life is hard… like in the gym when we are lifting heavy. Throughout this book, we will study God's word and His teachings. His son, Jesus, carried out His father's will and we continue to learn by His example. The *Focus on the Lift* exercises within each chapter will help us apply the chapter lessons and advice to our own life situations.

Accountability partners...
In addition to building trust within a relationship, when we are working to achieve a goal – whether physical, intellectual, or spiritual - we need to identify an "Accountability Partner." This individual is someone you trust who will encourage you to stay on point as you stretch yourself to achieve more. Are there people in your life who count on you to be the strong one in the midst of turmoil? How do you gather the strength? Who is your rock? Contemplate the following verses. What images come to mind as you say each verse out loud?

I can do all things through Him who strengthens me. [Philippians 4:13]

The LORD is my strength and song, And He has become my salvation; This is my God, and I will praise Him; My father's God, and I will extol Him. [Exodus 15:2]

My God, my rock, in whom I take refuge, My shield and the horn of my salvation, my stronghold and my refuge; My savior, You save me from violence. [2Samuel 22:3]

For we rejoice when we ourselves are weak but you are strong; this we also pray for, that you be made complete. [2Corinthians 13:9]

And without faith it is impossible to please *Him*, for he who comes to God must believe that He is and *that* He is a rewarder of those who seek Him. [Hebrews 11:6]

And we know that God causes all things to work together for good to those who love God, to those who are called according to His purpose. [Romans 8:28]

So, each scripture tells us that God is our source of strength and direction. Further, think about this idea: We are being called to be accountable to each other and to be accountable to God.

∆∆∆∆∆   *Focus on the Lift*   ∆∆∆∆∆

In *U R Titanium,* we are learning to follow God's lead in our daily workouts … strength training… to trust His guidance, timing, and build upon His path of perseverance one step at a time. As we begin this building process, let's examine our current experiences and changes we are seeking. What is "change"? This very simply stated, yet complex concept, has been top of mind for me while writing this book. Is change bad? No, not necessarily… some changes seem to have negative consequences, but some changes can actually produce positive results… maybe not immediately, but in the long run. What changes are you experiencing in your life? Write those down. Then, lift them up to God. Pray for insight and direction. God's plan for your life is in the works. Be open to His leadings and introductions to opportunities that you had never even dreamed of or considered as a possibility. We say, "Thank you, Lord, for the changes and improvements in our lives."

***

Walking by faith…
At times, we might have doubts about the possibility and probability that we can actually achieve what we are feeling called to do. Furthermore, as the verses on pages 3-4 remind us, we need to recognize God as our source of strength while working to capture the faith - the belief that with Him guiding us, we can do it! One day, I was talking with one of our church Pastors, Judy West, about spiritual gifts. She and I were sharing stories about current projects and times when we unexpectedly would meet the right person at the right time to help us take the next step toward the goal line. And, how it requires having strong faith in God and His plan to help us continue on the hard days. Admittedly, like in all of the true life stories in my first book, *Navigate with God*,[1] it feels like I get called to step out of my comfort zone fairly regularly. So, during a recent conversation with Judy, she said, "Ginny, I believe you have the gift of apostleship." I replied, "Well, I'm no Matthew, Mark, Luke, or John!" She responded, "That's not what I mean. The gift of apostleship means that you are not afraid to take a leap of faith… to lead never-before-done projects… to work outside your own comfort zone when it feels as though God is calling you to do so." Then, she reminded me of some of the initiatives I have helped launch. Something to think about…

Days come and go…
Months passed and I was still working on the new project ideas that Judy and I had been discussing. And, with the passage of time and not making much progress on anything, in my opinion, I kept remembering some past projects that launched well, but then ended when I moved on to work with another organization. Those memories invaded my waking hours, so I was losing my positive attitude… like I was not going to successfully complete any of the tasks… like I was failing.

And, then it happened…
God placed someone in my path to deliver His encouraging words. One Sunday, a local Pastor named David Hawkins was teaching at our church. David's message was about not focusing on past failures, but

rather looking ahead to recognize what God is calling you to do to grow His kingdom. He spoke of the reasons and blame for failing at a task on the spectrum from "deviant behavior" to "exploratory actions."[2] It felt as though David was speaking directly to me! Back to Judy's words… "not being afraid to exercise the gift of apostleship" when God is calling you to show up and explore new ministry ideas so that He can show out. We are not at fault for having to do some re-work on new ideas when we are working as exploratory leaders… leading others toward God.

Now, remember this…
"Know that He is God and when we are weak, He is strong." [2Corinthians 13:9] Let's continue to pray for strength through our weakness and gleaning of wisdom through our search for answers.

ΔΔΔΔΔ   *Focus on the Lift*   ΔΔΔΔΔ

Each day, every one of us has demands placed upon us… on our time… on our patience… on our tolerance… on our intellect… on our emotions… on our flexibility. This being said, let's think about the ways in which we react to the demands in our lives. At the end of the day, for the next seven days, write down the list of activities in which you were involved on that day. Then, next to each activity, write a brief description of the horizontal interactions with other people you experienced while working to complete the tasks. Next, write down the reactions you displayed and comments you voiced while communicating with others during those interactions. At the conclusion of this seven-day exercise, take some quiet time to review and reflect on your written comments from each day. How did you react to the daily demands placed upon you? Is there a pattern? Is it positive or negative? Is change needed?

***

In need of a Project Management Wake-up call…
We have all heard the phrase, "Life goes on." When we are trying to find the strength to deal with difficult situations in our lives, 1 Thessalonians 5:16-18 instructs us to: "Rejoice always; pray without ceasing; in everything give thanks; for this is God's will for you in Christ Jesus." As I continue to pray for daily guidance from both a personal and a global perspective, I will share a recent moment of revelation with you: through the tears and grief over losses that were completely out of my realm of control. There came a particular day when I realized that I was in need of a spiritual wake-up call in my life… again. Have you ever experienced that feeling? While working to burn the candle at both ends with tasks that I considered to be essential for sustainable "productivity," but in my "busy-ness" of day to day life, I was actually engaging in daily "activity" rather than productivity… for myself… for others… for God? Let's think about this for a moment: are we focusing each day on what time management experts refer to as "A –level" priorities… what I like to call "G-level," i.e., God-level priorities, or are we allowing less important tasks to infiltrate our conscious hours? That question can be a tough one to answer. Sometimes, we can become so focused on our daily tasks that we forget to look up from our toil to seek the bigger picture of our life purpose. Let's take a moment right now to prayerfully ask God to help up focus on the "To Do" list that He has prepared for us.

Do you arise each day with rejoicing or regret…?
I think I was falling out of touch with Jesus' example of nurturing a productive spirit-filled existence, while I believed myself to be striving to travel the journey that God had laid before us. Allow me to explain. Each day, instead of awakening in the morning with thoughts of thanks and praise for a new day, I was arising with worry over all of the tasks that I was expected to complete that day and the projects still left undone from the previous day. At the end of each day, I would try to go to sleep (unless I was working all night) – not giving thanks to God for the gifts and joys in my life that He had given me – but rather I would close my eyes with a sigh of relief that I had made it through another

day and then worry about what would happen the next day... if only I could just relax. This fearful feeling was becoming all too familiar – like in June of the year 2000, when I was nearly killed by a wrong-way driver on the interstate. At that time, I had lost spiritual direction in my life, and then losing the use of three limbs due to the car wreck caused me to stop... literally... and let God teach me about His constant presence, love, healing, and gift of grace. What a spiritual wake-up call that was! I had - and still have - so much to learn... insights to glean as we persevere... learning to walk, again... and learning to live, again. Are you in need of a life-strengthening spiritual wake-up call?

ΔΔΔΔΔ *Focus on the Lift* ΔΔΔΔΔ

What stresses are on your life right now? All of us can answer that question with at least two items. Write down your list of stresses, sign it, and place it in an envelope (or just fold it if you do not have one handy). Now, take two minutes to lift up your list in prayer to God, our Father, and ask Him to carry you and help you see the opportunities in your list of stresses. Ask Him to help you learn how to lean on Him and become aware of His direction in handling your stresses so that the items on your list do not take you away from God and His Son, but rather bring you closer to Them. There are family members and friends in your life who want to be emotionally closer to you, but they feel distant from you right now because you are distracted. Next, tuck the list into the back of your Bible... behind the Book of Revelations. With continued prayer, study of God's Word, and seeking His direction, you will experience an "Aha moment" of insight where God will be guiding and you will be following. Those "aha moments" can be quite exhilarating. They can make you feel like the solution has been right before you for some time and you never before realized it. God is pointing it out to you and leading you on the path of expanded awareness of His presence.

***

Changing course… Looking for the lighthouse…
Think about this: Our journey through life is parallel to that of an ocean voyage, where we try to keep the horizon in view so that we do not become disoriented – and that can be challenging at times. As we try to navigate the waters of life, particular circumstances can obscure our perspective… almost as if a fog has rolled in… sometimes patchy and sometimes dense. Ask God to help you see His purpose for your life more clearly. In *U R Titanium*, we will experience ways to "lift the veil of fog" from our lives and see the light, i.e., see more clearly the path and purpose God has for us to follow. God put Jesus in our lives as a lighthouse to help us navigate safely through the fog. Have you recognized and received God's light? Seek the lighthouse. He is seeking you. John 8:12 speaks of this light: "Then Jesus again spoke to them, saying, 'I am the Light of the world; he who follows Me will not walk in the darkness, but will have the Light of life.'" As you prayerfully seek and accept God's ever-constant presence in your life, His words and guidance will begin to resonate within and through you.

While we prayerfully begin to lift the veil of fog and look at our lives a little more closely each day, how can we begin to respond to this calling when our lives are cluttered and we do not know what to keep and what to throw away?

Taking inventory…
When teaching students about physical inventory management and internal controls, we talk about inventory cost flow assumptions and processes for safeguarding the assets. Be that the case, in this chapter we are talking about a different kind of inventory. We will call it "spiritual inventory." Periodically, I ask God to help me take a spiritual inventory of my life's priorities and intentions. Then, I ask Him to show me which tasks to embrace and which ones to discard. This spiritual exercise can be both unburdening and revealing. As God leads me through this "spiritual spring cleaning," I often feel called to look at life's situations from a new perspective… through a different lens. I find that this is not always easy to do because it requires me to stop… and think. Did

I say "stop"? Those of you who know me or have read my other books, know that I like to experience each day at the "speed of life," while trying to meet all demands. We all have daily responsibilities in our lives… and as we witness the changes and challenges present in today's world, meeting our own demands can seem impossible at times. Global economic strife, territorial battles, political disputes, and environmental decay are current issues which can intensify what we perceive to be our own struggles. Referring back to the idea of "spiritual inventory," let's prayerfully seek to know God and His purposes for our lives.

∆∆∆∆∆   *Focus on the Lift*   ∆∆∆∆∆

Spiritual inventory…
The purpose of this exercise is for you to ask God to help you take inventory of your spiritual life. Think about the time you spend each day exercising your spiritual beliefs. As in Matthew 6:3, do you work for God without the left hand knowing what the right hand is doing? Or boasting about it? At church? At work? How much time do you spend in God's word each day?

Next, write the following three column headings on a sheet of paper.

<u>Date</u>   <u>Action</u>   <u>Words</u>

Then, for the next eight days, fill in the columns with brief descriptions of the times when you believe that you were exercising your spiritual beliefs. After the eighth day, review the list and reflect on each activity. Was each task purposeful for God?

***

New perspective…
Do you ever feel the need to get down below the roots and simplify your own life? When we can do that, it helps us put life's complexities into better perspective. First, let's think about how nature's roots experience

seasonal growth and maturation. How do the roots of a tree receive nourishment so that they in turn can be the conduit for life-sustaining nourishment to the tree growing above the earth's surface? Nutrients can only reach the roots if the soil is of the necessary type and weeds are not blocking the pathway. How does this analogy relate to the roots of our lives? Think about this… what activities in your life are life-giving and which are life-suppressing?

In *U R Titanium*, we are learning how to view our lives – and changes in our lives – with a new perspective and focus on God's purpose. Author Rick Warren in his book, *Purpose Driven Life,* tells us that "we must be selective to be effective, and that lets us concentrate on what's important."[3] That is, we need to ask God to help us write our prioritized task list as we seek to understand His direction in our lives… each moment of each day.

We are all human and we tend to get so focused on daily activity, that we can mistake works of this world as spiritual progress on the road to eternal life in the kingdom of heaven. In James 2:26, we learn "For just as the body without the spirit is dead, so also faith without works is dead." So, we are called to have faith and synergistically share that faith with others through discipleship, advocacy, and action.

∆∆∆∆∆   *Focus on the Lift*   ∆∆∆∆∆

Go outside if you physically can… otherwise seek the nearest window, and witness God's presence in nature. Take ten minutes out of your busy day to feel God's nearness. Write down your thoughts and feelings… what is God showing you?

Which season are you experiencing? In nature? In life?

***

Ginny W. Frings, Ph.D.

Joy in the Journey...

Do you ever feel alone? Even during times when there are people present in our lives... within reach of a phone call... an e-mail... a text message... or a walk into the next room... we can still feel alone. Our existence here on earth is filled with seasons. These seasons take many forms – physical, emotional, relational, familial, intellectual, and spiritual. As I am writing this chapter, I just now glanced through the window in my office and noticed the squirrels hurriedly gathering nuts in the grass and venturing to the ends of tree branches, while seeking stores of sustenance for their impending winter survival. The beautifully colored leaves are falling from the trees and the temperatures are dropping to near-freezing, so the squirrels are in their season of preparation. While witnessing their endeavors, I began to recollect on the seasons in my life... friendships... adventures... challenges... opportunities. Then, I began to think about how busy life can get and the choices we make about how to spend our time – both demands on our time and discretionary use of our time each day. I was recently talking with a friend about how I used to have more time to spend with friends – have lunch, go for a walk, get together and take the children to the playground for a few hours. Was it that I actually "had" more time in my schedule or did I "make the decision to have" more time in my schedule... I think it was the latter.

Since this revelation, I began praying about time management and life management. I need to learn, again, how to build and nourish lasting friendships. With the personality of a "people-person," the journey as an author has been both interesting and challenging when moving to a new location and working to write a book while trying to build new friendships. I am asking God for His guidance. The leaves are glorious in this season and we are preparing for the purity of the new-fallen snow soon to come... can't wait to make a snow angel for Him.

There is a song by Michael Card entitled "Joy in the Journey"[4] where he sings about finding the path we should follow in life and "living in" the joys that we experience along the way... either small or palatial in stature… thanking God for His care and abundance of love. Even when times in our lives are difficult… or appear to be difficult… ask God to carry you and help you to acknowledge the joy of His presence.

God is ever-present…
Now, let's pause to more deeply reflect on God's presence in our lives. Think about His unconditional love for us and those we love. We need to drill deeper into the bedrock of our beliefs and build a foundation with God that will help us navigate through the challenges we are experiencing. God's love is constant. He is and will be ever present in our lives. Ask Him to help you see His existence more clearly. So many of us have spiritual cataracts where our view of God has become fogged with worries and concerns about tangible matters. Lift those worries and concerns up to God and experience what I call "silent reassurance" where we submit control to God and our job is to live in His grace and be witnesses for His abundant love, mercy, and forgiveness.

Text me…
Let's admit it – communication is key to building any relationship. In today's world, with technology literally at our fingertips, we often rely on what I call "passive" communication to schedule meetings, lunch dates, and even phone calls. We text: "Is now good to talk?" I am guilty of this… my friends know that I am terrible at checking voicemails… text me when you want to talk. The fact is though, that we need to use our God-given voices to talk more, that is, engage in "active" communication. Phone calls with FaceTime $_{TM,}$ Skype $_{TM,}$ and other technologies allow people to communicate face to face without having to be in the same room or even on the same continent! That's awesome!

Instant messaging with God…
<u>The God-directed lessons about purpose in our journey here on earth and how we can find the path to everlasting life still continue to come on a daily basis for us to receive into our lives, if we will allow ourselves to be open to embracing God's messages to us.</u> We IM (instant message) each other all day long. When you send up instant messages to God

(prayers), ask Him to share His instant messages with you! And, know that there is always excellent reception (4G… For God) and no texting limits!

ΔΔΔΔΔ   *Focus on the Lift*   ΔΔΔΔΔ

Now, on paper, write a text message to God and prayerfully ask Him to respond. What do you want to say to Him? Then, be S-I-L-E-N-T and L-I-S-T-E-N for His reply.

***

Let God prepare the way…
Before we explore more deeply the path and purpose which God is calling us to follow, let's invite God and His Son into our lives as ever-present directors of our steps and decisions. Remember, in Jeremiah 10:23 we learn: "I know, O LORD, that a man's way is not in himself, Nor is it in a man who walks to direct his steps."

And,

John 14:6
"Jesus said to him, 'I am the way, and the truth, and the life; no one comes to the Father but through Me.'" Let's pray to journey through this life on the path to eternal life with the Father as our guide. He will prepare the way.

Let God make ready the way for you to journey on the path to His grace and abundant love. He is waiting for you. Invite Him into your life. Let's begin right now learning how to take the next step into our own *Titanium Transformation* with God as our guide… He's our personal trainer!

△△△△△   *Focus on the Lift*   △△△△△

So, now with the demands and stresses of life, many of us are feeling the pull to be more than we can humanly be while working through situations that have been put upon us… whether relegated by another or intentionally brought about by our own design. Let's pray about this: in your hours of consciousness each day, what is currently "top of mind" for you? What would God see as "top of mind important" for you in this season of your life? Write down your list and then pray about what God's task list for your life might look like.

***

Realize…
So far in this book, we have been working to realize that we can trust God to carry and guide us. Pray with me right now. Lord, thank you for your leadership in my life. Thank you for showing me the way into your heart. I trust you, Lord. Please forgive me for the times when I have gone astray. Help me to become someone whom You can trust to carry out Your will. Teach me. I love you, Lord. Amen.

Chapter 2
Incentives

"Obstacles don't have to stop you. If you run into a wall, don't turn around and give up. Figure out how to climb it, go through it, or work around it." Michael Jordan

INCENTIVES
by Albert Cloudy

The best at what you do
Hard work and consistency
Catches eyes of the higher power
Because you stick out with your talent
Comes with incentives
A prize, a raise, a gift
Rewards for you that thrives and causes notice
A confidence booster
Cause you to work in tremendous ways
Excel and show out knowing the perks
Brings out the inner you that you didn't know
Surprise you and others
Continue down the road to success.

©2016 Albert Cloudy. All rights reserved. Used with permission.

Hope…

So we could say that change is an incentive to change. Circular reasoning? Indeed, it is not. Changes that happen to us often act as incentive to change something within us. And, as we experience times in our lives when we must adapt to circumstances, sometimes it can feel like we are at the end of our rope and we just can't take it anymore. I felt that way after the car wreck when doctors were saying that I might never walk, again. But, family and friends were trying to encourage me to try anyway. Of course, they all knew how stubborn I was… still am. I nearly died in that head-on collision, but for some reason God saved my life… awaking seven days later on a ventilator… then in months to come existing in a wheelchair… and six more years of surgeries. I was curious as to why I was still alive. God has a plan. Recently, I was talking with a friend about this very idea. When bad things happen, why do some people keep pushing ahead trying to find a way to get through it, while others just give up. This chapter is about incentives. What drives you to get up and show up? My friend, Kim Vetter, MBA, MA, LPC, and I were having lunch the other day and this question entered the conversation. What is it? What is the incentive factor that is present to some of us and missing for others? Kim works as a Christian counselor in St. Louis. Her clientele runs the spectrum from adolescents to seniors. Her response to my question: "Hope. When people lose hope, they lose their incentive to go on. They give up. But, when we ask God to help us have hope - the hope that things will get better, He gives us the hope that we can find our way through this mess and find joy in life again one day." Kim also says that often it is the people surrounding the person who has lost hope who can have the greatest impact on the person's recovery from the feeling of hopelessness. We can help people around us surmount the problems in their lives and move on to another and better season of life – one in which they have the hope, confidence, and better self-esteem - all God-centered… to not just exist, but rather to thrive. Let's prayerfully contemplate the following verses:

"Therefore, having been justified by faith, we have peace with God through our Lord Jesus Christ, through whom also we have obtained our introduction by faith into this grace in which we stand; and we exult in hope of the glory of God. And not only this, but we also exult in our tribulations, knowing that tribulation brings about perseverance; and perseverance, proven character; and proven character, hope; and hope does not disappoint, because the love of God has been poured out within our hearts through the Holy Spirit who was given to us." [Romans 5:1-5]

Right now, take a moment to reflect on the idea of "hope." What images come to mind?

Incentives to become stronger…
Here is the poem that a local school district liaison sent to me, wanting to get a published author's thoughts on this student's work… the student is Albert Cloudy… at the time he was a high school Senior:

I Am
by Albert Cloudy

I am me
I am me
Had my troubles in the beginning
Got on track and now my world's spinning
Doors are opening
With lots of opportunities to choose
so many possibilities it's hard to lose
Words cannot express
what this program has done for me
Bussed from the city and out to the county
Takes a toll physically and mentally
but the education is worth it, most definitely

More resources given to us every day
While other schools barely have a place to play
I am lucky that I've entered the doors to success
You, me, and all of the others should count ourselves blessed

U R Titanium

Activities that we can attend with a little bit of help
Always have someone to depend on when there's no one else
Friends I've made from different cultures and backgrounds
Love, support, and guidance constantly surrounds
With this occurrence I have a lot to show for
They left me with a thirst that's got me wanting more for
Adults on my side, ready to lend a helping hand
Or willing to motivate, express ideas, take a stand

This school, this place, my second home
Pushed me forward through every hardship I've known
Each day made it apparent I was not alone.

Take time to really think about where you would be
If wasn't for the help of the V-I-C-C
Maybe another school, you would make lots of friends
Friends who in front of, you'd have to pretend
An education, too, but one that's harder to grasp
Memories that'd fade and impressions that wouldn't last

Only a few more steps
And we've made it to the other side
Glad we stood in the moment;
Glad we put forth the time

Not saying we've had it easy or it didn't take sweat
All the hard work and adversity made us our best
Our very best to stroll across the graduation stage
Our very best to start the next chapter, the next page
… in our lives

So, thank you to those who made it all possible
For taking a risk on me, you're truly phenomenal
You've given me a debt, I'll never be able to repay
But, please know in your heart, it's me you have saved

Ginny W. Frings, Ph.D.

I am me
Was not so good at the beginning
Now a future so bright; I'm destined for winning.
Thank you

©2016 Albert Cloudy. All rights reserved. Used with permission.

My first reaction was "Wow! This student is truly a poet… the hook of the intro lines… the talk of the challenge… the emotion… the grasping for the life line in seeking a change… the call to action… the gratitude for this unique opportunity (V-I-C-C programs which brought him into a nourishing educational environment) … all very well said, Mr. Albert Cloudy." Throughout the pages of this book, Albert's poems will engage, embrace, and inspire you to become stronger and truer to your calling.

Looking to scripture for strength, we can embrace the teaching and encouragement when we spend time in God's Word. We can achieve spiritual energy through resting in God's presence and asking Him about when we should take the next step. Pray Isaiah 40:31 with me. Then, rest for a few moments… relax with Jesus… and feel God's presence and strength flow through you. Isaiah 40:31 teaches of the strength we gain when walking with Jesus:

Yet those who wait for the LORD
Will gain new strength;
They will mount up *with* wings like eagles,
They will run and not get tired,
They will walk and not become weary.

Expect change to occur…
The world continuously experiences change on many facets. Physical changes to the earth's core and atmosphere (even the theory of global warming) are far-reaching and endeavors to "go green" will hopefully delay the decay. Where are we as a species leaving our footprints… carbon? ecological? Financially, the markets in many parts of the world

experience turbulence fairly regularly. Wars and territorial disputes over property rights still happen – some resulting in revolutions and transfers of power. Where is all of this leading? As individuals we do not know, but as a collective body of God we can weather the changes and make a difference while we are here on earth.

"I can't change the direction of the wind, but I can adjust my sails to always reach my destination." Jimmy Dean

Sometimes we must modify the method to reach our next milestone...
Some of us say, "Keep everything the same. Don't rock my boat!" Is that truly possible? My father-in-law, Chris Frings, would say:

"It used to be known that: if everyone always does what they have always done, then they will always get what they have always gotten. Nowadays, if everyone does what they have always done, they will get left out!"

Let's not get left out or left behind. Let's work through our challenges and persevere to the finish line. Remember: Hebrews 12 encourages us. Hebrews 12:1 teaches us to stay in the life race… to persevere on the path… in a cloud of witnesses. The storm will pass. God will walk with you through your circumstances and carry you when you feel you cannot cross the chasm by yourself.

> *Jesus, the Example*
>
> Therefore, since we have so great a cloud of witnesses surrounding us, let us also lay aside every encumbrance and the sin which so easily entangles us, and let us run with endurance the race that is set before us, fixing our eyes on Jesus, the author and perfecter of faith, who for the joy set before Him endured the cross, despising the shame, and has sat down at the right hand of the throne of God. For consider Him who has endured such hostility by sinners against Himself, so that you will not grow weary and lose heart. [Hebrews 12:1-3]

Let us prayerfully continue on the path of perseverance… learning to adapt with the changes along the way. Persevering and working to be flexible, i.e., adaptable to varying circumstances, requires us to expend energy – mental, physical, emotional, and spiritual.

∆∆∆∆ *Focus on the Lift* ∆∆∆∆

This exercise involves contemplating your next move toward the successful completion of your goal. Open your mind and ponder this scene…

Sunrise was beautiful this morning… lighting your path toward your next milestone… yes… very cool. We are all called to make the most of each moment of each day… just like witnessing the dolphins each morning finding the catch of the day… seeing the sea turtles swimming into their new Atlantic home… and the dolphins once again breaking the water's surface at sunset… sweet… beautiful blessings. Come on… Let's go seek those next goals. For a few moments, sit quietly to ponder a goal on which you are currently working to achieve.

Like we say at Team M.O.V.E… Exercise where you're at… in your life journey… physically… mentally… spiritually… Let's Do This. Keep your mind on what matters.

***

Water from a rock?...
In church this morning, the pastor was talking about Moses and his experience in the wilderness where there was no water for him and his fellow travelers. His followers were questioning his leadership… asking Moses why he had brought them and their flocks to this place of desolation.

Water in the Rock

Then all the congregation of the sons of Israel journeyed by stages from the wilderness of Sin, according to the command of the LORD, and camped at Rephidim, and there was no water for the people to drink.

Therefore the people quarreled with Moses and said, "Give us water that we may drink " And Moses said to them, "Why do you quarrel with me? Why do you test the LORD?"

But the people thirsted there for water; and they grumbled against Moses and said, "Why, now, have you brought us up from Egypt, to kill us and our children and our livestock with thirst?"

So Moses cried out to the LORD, saying, "What shall I do to this people? A little more and they will stone me."

Then the LORD said to Moses, "Pass before the people and take with you some of the elders of Israel; and take in your hand your staff with which you struck the Nile, and go.

"Behold, I will stand before you there on the rock at Horeb; and you shall strike the rock, and water will come out of it, that the people may drink." And Moses did so in the sight of the elders of Israel.

He named the place Massah and Meribah because of the quarrel of the sons of Israel, and because they tested the LORD, saying, "Is the LORD among us, or not?" (Exodus 17: 1-7)

Question: What did Moses do when His followers questioned the path? *Answer:* He went to God with the problem, shared his theory that the crowds were about ready to stone him for bringing them to such desolation, and basically cried out to God: "What should I do? Please advise!" Moses became silent to await the Lord's answer. He then heeded God's reply, did exactly what he was asked to do, and water sprang forth from a rock... enough to sufficiently quench the travelers' thirst. Notice when you read the passage above, that the "staff" with which God asks Moses to strike the rock is the same staff he used to strike the Nile. And, notice that Moses still had that staff with him. Lesson: We will be given and learn how to use the tools we need to emerge from life's dilemmas. Catalogue those tools and experiences because God may call upon you to use them again in the future.

Looking at Moses and his relationship with the Lord, we see unconditional love and reliance. My question to you: when problems arose, did Moses "build a wall against the difficulty" or "build a windmill of hope by seeking God's wisdom and direction" so that he could be a more effective leader for God? I think you already know the answer to that question.

"When the wind blows the cradle will rock..."[1] [from Brahm's Lullaby]
Through our own lives, have we learned to seek out God when the path seems unclear? Or, do we put on blinders and keep trudging through the darkened valley by ourselves in search of the mountain vantage point where we hope to get a view of the upcoming trail and horizon? But, as we reach the summit, what if there's cloud cover, i.e., circumstances, people, or obstacles obstructing the view? How do we proceed? Are we on the right path? The correct summit? Where am I going with this line of questioning you are probably wondering... Here it is. When seeking direction in our lives, if we go ahead and send out our S.O.S. to God and ask Him to guide us, He will carry us when needed, even when we are traveling upon a seemingly treacherous path. He will show us the way!

Building a strong foundation...mentally... physically... spiritually
As you work through the *Focus on the Lift* exercises in this book, you are experiencing the opportunity to build your own stronghold of lessons and scriptures to weave into your own life journey and hone your

awareness of God, Jesus, and the Holy Spirit's presence. They are there for you and always listening. Call out to Them. Build your life on a firm foundation – God's word. Be filled with His grace, always knowing that He is with you. He will give you the strength and gifts needed to work through your challenges. Just ask Him. Now, let's ponder this message on foundations…

"Why do you call Me, 'Lord, Lord,' and do not do what I say? Everyone who comes to Me and hears My words and acts on them, I will show you whom he is like: he is like a man building a house, who dug deep and laid a foundation on the rock; and when a flood occurred, the torrent burst against that house and could not shake it, because it had been well built. "But the one who has heard and has not acted accordingly, is like a man who built a house on the ground without any foundation; and the torrent burst against it and immediately it collapsed, and the ruin of that house was great."[Luke 6:46-49]

And, then Matthew 7:24 teaches us about the importance of fortifying life's foundations.

"Therefore everyone who hears these words of Mine and acts on them, may be compared to a wise man who built his house on the rock."

△△△△△ *Focus on the Lift* △△△△△

Let's continue our strength-building journey with this *Focus on the Lift* exercise. Step 1: Close your eyes and ask God for a few moments of calmness. Step 2: Praise God for all of the blessings in your life. Step 3: Think of two challenges or obstacles which you feel are causing stress and disturbance in your life. Step 4: Open your eyes. On a piece of paper, draw a picture of a cross – however you imagine it… large… small… colorful or not… on a mountain… near the ocean… Use your imagination. Step 5: Now, write those challenges and obstacles below the base of your cross. If there are more things you want to write there, go ahead and do it. You are now laying your worries at the foot of the cross. Step 6: Close your eyes and thank God for unburdening you through His abundant grace and mercy. He loves you. Keep your Cross drawing. Later in the book, we will refer back to this exercise.

***

Personal Mission Statement…
So, when we are thinking about working toward a goal, we want to know what attributes – physical – mental – spiritual - are required for achieving success. And, what is the incentive for taking on the challenge… let's pause for a moment. What is the reason for your pursuit? Are you on some type of "mission" perhaps?

∆∆∆∆∆   *Focus on the Lift*   ∆∆∆∆∆

When leading programs on achieving goals, I talk with audiences about not only the vision and mission statement for their company or organization, but also their own personal vision and mission statements. What is God calling them to do and how are they responding to His call? To illustrate, think about and write a few sentences about each of these phrases:

- Who you are
- Why you exist
- What you intend to do
- Where you are going
- How you plan to get there
- When you are going to arrive
- And Sooooo, when are you going to arrive? All in God's timing!

State each phrase in the form of a question, and then think about your answers to these questions. You are beginning to shape your own personal strength-building exercise routine that we will be developing throughout the pages of this book.

Next, pray about the phrases and your responses, and then ask God to lead you to His intentions. Write down the ideas that come to mind as you pray about God's direction for your life.

As you pray about your mission statement, make six columns on a sheet of paper. Then, write these column headings: WHO; WHY; WHAT; WHERE; HOW and WHEN. Write down your thoughts about WHO you are, WHY you exist, WHAT you intend to do, WHERE you are going, HOW you plan to get there, and WHEN you will arrive… with God as your guide. Ask Him, and He will either tell you or place people and ideas in your path that are pieces to fulfilling God's life puzzle for you. For example, when I gave my first motivational talk since the car wreck on May 17, 2001, I wanted to have a handout for the program. So, I designed a bookmark which outlined the talk and gave the audience members a nice keepsake of the message. "A bookmark - that's different. I like it," audience members would say. Then, through the years I have customized a bookmark for every speaking engagement… hundreds… all colors of the rainbow… different messages for each program. Then, one day while preparing for a talk in 2008 (after the publication of my first book), I realized that I finally had "a book to go with the bookmark" that I was designing for my next audience. It was a *Golden Moment* of revelation and realization that God knew I would one day be an author. Remember the quote: "God does not call the qualified. He qualifies the called." [Author unknown] Pray about that idea… God will lead you in pursuit of your calling.

Now, let's continue writing the segments of your mission statement. Ask God for direction and guidance for charting alternative courses of action when changes occur. We will revisit this exercise in Chapter 8 when we talk about what we really mean by strength.

***

Did you ever have a day where…
Each day is different. No sequence of events in a twenty four hour day is exactly the same as the events of the previous day. Change comes in all sizes and frequencies. Pray about this question: Temporally, how do you handle unexpected change? Do you stiffen in rebellion or embrace the difference in plans as an opportunity?

Did you ever have a day where you began the day feeling that you had everything under control and your schedule appeared to be logistically reasonable… i.e., not "really" needing to be two places at once… almost, but you knew that you could make everything work and keep all of your commitments? And, knowing that when you arrived back home that evening there would still be at least five loads of laundry to wash and two loads of dishes to do after getting the family settled down for a good night's sleep. I did: yesterday.

Expect the unexpected?...
As I was living at the "speed of life" yesterday, all the details of reality seemed to be handled. Then, I received an out-of-the-blue phone call from an old friend. It was nice to catch up on news. Then, another phone call came about a problem that I thought had been solved, and then there was a voice mail waiting for me after running around all day working to fulfill "the schedule" that had seemed so do-able that morning. As I was dialing the number to return the phone call, I was trying to have a positive attitude, but deep down I knew that the person on the other end was probably going to yell at me about something over which I had no control (the tone of the voice mail was my clue). I listened to the rather irate person on the other end telling me that the solutions I had suggested and tried to implement were inadequate for the situation. The conversation continued and that person proceeded to recall similar difficult experiences where, again, the path had been unclear and my presence had been seen as an intrusion. But, ultimately God handled the situation to everyone's satisfaction. Why did this person feel compelled to only mention the past problems and not the solutions that had unfolded before our eyes? As I continued to listen,

I was praying about how to handle this call and this person. Have you ever felt like that?

This particular situation brought to mind a song performed by Casting Crowns entitled "Voice of Truth" [2] where they talk about being out of one's comfort zone and seeking God's voice rather than internalizing other people's judgments and criticisms, like people telling you that you can't do it… saying that you will fail. Those are the types of comments I was hearing from the person on the other end of the phone call… just earthly human negativity. As I politely listened to this individual, I was prayerfully seeking God's voice and guidance while trying to circumvent the pessimism of the other individual. We are working through the situation with God's guidance… Jesus is walking with us and carrying us when needed… one step at a time.

Trying not to stumble…
Psalm 91 teaches us that God is with us. We need to acknowledge His presence and He will lift us up so that we do not "strike our foot against a stone." Pray these verses from Psalm 91 with me.

> I will say to the LORD, "My refuge and my fortress,
> My God, in whom I trust!"
> For it is He who delivers you from the snare of the trapper
> And from the deadly pestilence.
> He will cover you with His pinions,
> And under His wings you may seek refuge;
> His faithfulness is a shield and bulwark.
> You will not be afraid of the terror by night,
> Or of the arrow that flies by day;
> Of the pestilence that stalks in darkness,
> Or of the destruction that lays waste at noon.
> A thousand may fall at your side
> And ten thousand at your right hand,
> But it shall not approach you.
> You will only look on with your eyes

    And see the recompense of the wicked.
For you have made the LORD, my refuge,
    Even the Most High, your dwelling place.
No evil will befall you,
    Nor will any plague come near your tent.
For He will give His angels charge concerning you,
    To guard you in all your ways. [Psalm 91:2-11]

And, again, recall Isaiah 40:31 encourages us:

Yet those who wait for the LORD
Will gain new strength;
They will mount up with wings like eagles,
They will run and not get tired,
They will walk and not become weary.

Think about the challenges you are facing right now, or expect to be facing in the near future. Prayerfully ask God to give you strength and guidance. Seek His presence… His face… His leading. Then try to be aware. He will answer your prayers… in the people you meet… opportunities that arise… new ideas that suddenly come to mind… scriptures that draw your attention. Seek to be aware of His presence in your life. Agree to trust Him.

Now, the Declaration…
Having lived in many states across this nation, I always enjoyed learning about the history and development of each area – geographically, politically, agriculturally, economically, academically, culturally, and spiritually. While living on the east coast, we studied of revolutions and unifications within differing boundaries. While living on the west coast, it was interesting to learn the history of incentives for gold mining and development of later states joining the union. Now in St. Louis, the Gateway to the West, we are learning more about ancestors' migration and transformation across the nation. As leaders and historians become vocal about their intentions and direction, they often feel the need to

publically document their ideas on formation and re-formation. For example, according to Merriam-Webster, "manifesto" refers to "a written statement declaring publicly the intentions, motives, or views of its issuer."[3] While pondering this term one day and considering the realm of possibilities for speaking and writing about God's grace and mercy, I was reminded of Steven Curtis Chapman's song entitled "Declaration of Dependence,"[4] where he sings about our need to write our personal declaration of "dependence" on Christ. In a way, he makes us think about stepping back into the days when this country was founded on the principle "In God We Trust" upon the composition and signing of the original "U.S. Declaration of Independence." Interesting twist when we review history and the intentions of our founding fathers… calling upon God to help them colonize a new territory: "One nation under God, indivisible, with liberty and justice for all." [excerpt from United States of America Pledge of Allegiance] And, look where we have landed today.

ΔΔΔΔΔ   *Focus on the Lift* ΔΔΔΔΔ

Now is the time for each of us to revisit history and write a manifesto declaring unity, equality, humanity, and reliance on God. This introspective exercise has both "micro" - or internally spiritual - and "macro"- or far-reaching - implications: Write your own manifesto – what are your intentions and views? Vision? Values? For your life? For your community? Your company? Your state? Your nation? Your world? Write out your list for each location. Then, pray to God about your answers. Write down His messages to you.

Each day, we will continue to learn how to devote ourselves and time to dialoguing with God to strive toward implementing His holy plan. <u>Ask</u> God into your life. <u>Seek</u> His direction. <u>Praise</u> Him for His leading presence. We are talking about everlasting reliance on God in our everyday lives… through obstacles and trials…in times of sadness and times of happiness… like Steven Curtis Chapman's song "Declaration of Dependence."[5] Write your "Declaration of Dependence" on a piece of paper, beginning with: I, [name], declare my dependence on God… and continuing with ways in which you will invite God into your life.

***

"A bird doesn't sing because it has an answer, it sings because it has a song." – Maya Angelou

What are your incentives?
Solutions for overcoming challenges can be timely and timeless… with God's guidance. We are given experiences that we can use to learn about perseverance and spiritual growth. Pray about this idea and reflect on some adventures in your life where the lessons you learned appeared both timely and timeless… "and" not "versus." When I teach MBA courses on corporate governance and corporate social responsibility (CSR), we discuss theory and application of the four modes of CSR: philanthropic; compliance; risk management; and value-added. These levels of organizational responsibility can be applied to our spiritual lives. Ponder this… what level of commitment have you given to God and His work? Parallel the CSR hierarchy to this question. So, are you devoting some time to live God's Word and help others? On what level: Philanthropic? Compliance? Risk management? Value-added? That can be a difficult question to answer truthfully. Are many of us devoting the time and energy to growing God's Kingdom that we truly should be? Ask God to help you better manage your time… I am praying about this request right now.

Think about God's timing. In Galations 6:9, we learn "Let us not lose heart in doing good, for in due time we will reap if we do not grow weary." In due time… what does that mean? We do not have control over the timing of events such as the rising and setting of the sun… of the germination of flowers… of weather patterns… and unforeseen changes in our lives. Thinking about life, God truly is in control, and we are His instruments. What roles should we play? What are the incentives that lead us to recognize those roles? These questions bring the need for us to consider the spiritual gifts with which God has graced us. And, how can we best use our gifts and time to help ourselves and others handle life's changes and challenges?

Chapter 3

Time

"I don't have time for this!" [says one human to another]

Time: according to Merriam Webster, time is the measured or measurable period during which an action, process, or condition exists or continues; duration: a nonspatial continuum that is measured in terms of events which succeed one another from past through present to future. [1]

TIME
by Albert Cloudy

Being strong and having the strength to overcome
Is the key in life to make it through obstacles
But keep in mind these things don't come easy
Or with the snap of your finger it takes time
And while time is all you need live life to the fullest,
Life like there's no tomorrow and accomplish
And make it through everything life throws at you
Life is a test which needs to be passed
In time conquering that task is possible
Willing to do what is right and thrive
All greatness will come with a little time
But realize it just takes time.

©2016 Albert Cloudy. All rights reserved. Used with permission.

Sand to pearl… coal to diamond…
Picture the beauty of the sand… from sugar-white Gulf beaches to varying amber hues of the sand connecting the sun-kissed cliffs to the tides of the coastal oceans… the fun of building sand castles and the excitement of children as they scurry after a sand crab or pursue a seagull on the beach. And, what nourishing sea life are those cute little sand pipers retrieving with their beaks buried in the sand? Have you ever written the message "I love you" to someone special with a stick in the sand? As a grain of sand seemingly becomes a source of irritation to an oyster, the oyster gives it attention (smoothing) to alleviate discomfort and the tiny grain of sand ultimately becomes a beautiful pearl. Another phenomenon within nature is that of a piece of coal being transformed into a multi-faceted diamond. These processes take time…incentive… pressure.

Tick… tock…
So, is it correct for us to claim not to have "time" for something or someone? To claim ownership of time… when, in reality, we do not have control of a continuum which operates independently of us and our actions… inactions… and distractions? Actually, we have time for whatever we are being called to fulfill in God's plan. He - the creator of time - would not call you to complete a task for which you are not gifted with adequate time. This moment of clarity could lead us to change our perspective about "having" time, to rather "taking" the necessary time to do something… to communicate with someone… to help on a project… to stop and just breathe for a few minutes.

∆∆∆∆∆ Focus on the Lift ∆∆∆∆∆

As we ponder the activities which we must perform on a daily basis – oftentimes requiring us to multi-task – let's stop for a moment to make note of how much we think about the aspect of "time." What I mean is, how often are we more focused on the clock than on the task at hand? For example, when we are working out at the gym, I sometimes find myself watching the clock with the mindset of "let's just get through this" rather than focusing on each lift and which muscles are being tested. When that happens, my workout buddies will point out to me that I need to change my attitude because rushing through a workout with improper form can lead to sub-optimization and possible injury. This scenario is analogous to the way in which we handle tasks each day. If we were to focus more on the job to be done and become less distracted by the "clock"… including our smart phones… we could increase productivity while lowering stress levels. Let's put this hypothesis into action by identifying three tasks on which we need to make progress today. On a piece of paper, write a brief description of each agenda item and then write down the time of day when you are scheduled to work on each one. Next, put the paper away in a drawer where you will not come across it today. On the morning of the following day, retrieve the list of three items and review the progress made on each task while you sit quietly and prayerfully. Then, calmly and courageously ask God to help you be even more focused and productive on this new day. Continue to repeat this exercise each day until you feel confident that you are willing to allow God to direct your time because He is building up your focus while reducing your perceived pressures, leading you into a feeling of confident tranquility with the Holy Spirit.

***

Time is now… you are being called…
"Therefore I, the prisoner of the Lord, implore you to walk in a manner worthy of the calling with which you have been called, with all humility and gentleness, with patience, showing tolerance for one another in love, being diligent to preserve the unity of the Spirit in the bond of peace. *There is* one body and one Spirit, just as also you were called in one hope of your calling; one Lord, one faith, one baptism, one God and Father of all who is over all and through all and in all." [Ephesians 4:1-6]

Contemplate your own life and see the parallels between many facets of our lives and the seasons of nature. It's interesting when we hear the phrase "spiritual rebirth," and those of us who have survived near death experiences or tragic illnesses, understand the idea of rebirth through rehabilitation… spiritual rebirth as in seeing the world with a new perspective… emotional rebirth in prioritizing our lives… occupational or educational rebirth in seeing ways to restructure our work-life balance… familial rebirth in reconciliation and healing of dysfunctional relationships. What type(s) of rebirth are you seeking? Like 1Peter 1:3 teaches us: "Blessed be the God and Father of our Lord Jesus Christ, who according to His great mercy has caused us to be born again to a living hope through the resurrection of Jesus Christ from the dead,"

Steven Curtis Chapman's song, "God is God,"[2] is about surrendering your life to God and being reborn. The lyrics remind me of my experience of spiritual rebirth after the car wreck – sometimes we become broken in order to be healed. When Jesus was explaining rebirth to the disciples, their follow-up questions seemed to imply that they thought He meant "physical" rebirth from their mother's womb. Actually, Jesus meant spiritual rebirth into a life as a servant-leader.

Supply and demand…
As we move quickly through the activities of daily life… at the speed of life… we breathe a sigh of relief (if we have time to take a deep breath) at the successful execution of each duty, and then go on to the next. I am feeling stressed just thinking about it. What exactly is stress? Merriam Webster defines stress as: "the deformation caused in a body by such a force; a physical, chemical, or emotional factor that causes bodily or mental tension and may be a factor in disease causation; a state resulting from a stress; *especially* one of bodily or mental tension resulting from factors that tend to alter an existent equilibrium, e.g., job-related *stress.*"[3]

"Existent equilibrium" in economics, is the equilibrium which expresses the intersection of two curves, e.g., market is in equilibrium at the point where supply meets demand. Think about that concept. Does the "supply of you" equal the "demands that are being placed upon you" physically, emotionally, intellectually, and spiritually? I have felt "out of equilibrium" this week… like the *demands on me* have exceeded the *supply of me* lately. I was on my knees this morning asking God to guide me and our family on the path He envisions for us to follow. And, to help us focus on His plan, not our own human agendas.

The turmoil of the financial markets is adding "stressful <u>dis</u>equilibrium" to many consumers' lives these days. Financial worries are one of the leading causes for distressed marriages and relationships. Emotional taunting, abrupt comments, and deteriorating attitudes are plaguing many households during times of world economic implosion. How can we "arise from this relational decline"?

In chapter four of *Navigate with God,* [4] I led you through developing the feeling of "silent reassurance" in the presence of God. Let's sit quietly for a few moments and ask God to help us recognize Him in the here and now, as we ponder what it means to be reborn as a servant-leader for God.

Let's read the following scenario where Jesus explains the concept of rebirth to the scholar, Nicodemus:

"Now there was a man of the Pharisees, named Nicodemus, a ruler of the Jews;
this man came to Jesus by night and said to Him, "Rabbi, we know that You have come from God as a teacher; for no one can do these signs that You do unless God is with him."
Jesus answered and said to him, "Truly, truly, I say to you, unless one is born again he cannot see the kingdom of God."
Nicodemus said to Him, "How can a man be born when he is old? He cannot enter a second time into his mother's womb and be born, can he?"
Jesus answered, "Truly, truly, I say to you, unless one is born of water and the Spirit he cannot enter into the kingdom of God.
"That which is born of the flesh is flesh, and that which is born of the Spirit is spirit.

"Do not be amazed that I said to you, 'You must be born again.'

"The wind blows where it wishes and you hear the sound of it, but do not know where it comes from and where it is going; so is everyone who is born of the Spirit."

Nicodemus said to Him, "How can these things be?"

Jesus answered and said to him, "Are you the teacher of Israel and do not understand these things?

"Truly, truly, I say to you, we speak of what we know and testify of what we have seen, and you do not accept our testimony.

"If I told you earthly things and you do not believe, how will you believe if I tell you heavenly things?

"No one has ascended into heaven, but He who descended from heaven: the Son of Man.

"As Moses lifted up the serpent in the wilderness, even so must the Son of Man be lifted up;

so that whoever believes will in Him have eternal life.

"For God so loved the world, that He gave His only begotten Son, that whoever believes in Him shall not perish, but have eternal life.

"For God did not send the Son into the world to judge the world, but that the world might be saved through Him.

"He who believes in Him is not judged; he who does not believe has been judged already, because he has not believed in the name of the only begotten Son of God.

"This is the judgment, that the Light has come into the world, and men loved the darkness rather than the Light, for their deeds were evil.

"For everyone who does evil hates the Light, and does not come to the Light for fear that his deeds will be exposed.

"But he who practices the truth comes to the Light, so that his deeds may be manifested as having been wrought in God." [John 3:1-21]

ΔΔΔΔΔ *Focus on the Lift* ΔΔΔΔΔ

While studying Christ's life as annotated throughout the scriptures, we learn of His journey and dialogues with people around Him. He teaches us about the concept of "being born again," where we invite the Holy

Spirit to dwell within each of us. In doing so, we learn how to follow God's leadings each day. This rebirth opens the door for building a stronger relationship with the Trinity. And, we can ask Jesus to carry us when we don't see the next step in our own journey. So, we can apply this idea of rebirth to relationships within our lives. Pray about this question: In what areas of your life do you feel the need for rebirth?

***

When the winds of change blow, there are those who build walls and those who build windmills. [Chinese Proverb]

There are so many questions to which we all are seeking answers. Questions such as: Why must we "deal with" change? What does the future hold? And the familiar, yet often forbidden inquiry: Why me? We all experience a myriad of changes in our lives… ranging from dramatic to trivial, in the essences of: physical… emotional… relational… educational… spiritual… and occupational. Difficult economic times can exacerbate or seem to create difficulties in other areas of our lives. Sometimes, it feels like problems crash into our lives as though they are waves… and then the tide ebbs for a period of time… and then another set of waves rolls into shore.

Seasons of change…
Seasons are times when we can observe changes. We witness varying temperatures and weather patterns. We recognize differences in animal behavior, (for example, squirrels searching for and storing food for the winter, bears bulking up for hibernation, birds flying south for the winter… deer coming around in the spring seeking new growth… and changes in the trees each season.) But, what about our personal seasons of life? How do we define those experiences? In her book *Discovering God's Purpose for Your Life*,[5] Beth Moore talks of these times of change as "seasons" in our lives where we must learn how to "know Christ through the _____ season" - fill in here the description which best describes the types of challenges you are facing right now. In the

changing seasons of our lives, Beth teaches us that God has purpose for our experiences and we can know that He has great things planned for us. Can you relate? I know I can. We all have seasons of loss… of growth… of letting go… of gathering in. Right now is a season of knowing Christ through the rebirth… of our spiritual walk… ministry… careers… relationships. Thank you Beth, for sharing your wisdom and insights into the seasons of our lives and the need to seek Christ's presence through it all.

Setting the timing…
For those of us who like to restore classic cars, defining the optimal "ignition or spark timing" on an engine can sometimes be difficult. We measure the rpm at idle, and then work to set the timing where the ignition spark, the catalyst for combustion, occurs at the preferred rate and responsiveness. When you know either the timing at idle or the maximum advance at a given engine speed, and you have a good timing light, you will be better equipped to set the timing. When I was in high school, my Daddy (Neil Williamson) and I would work together on how to properly set the timing of my Mustang (1968 289 V8 light metallic green California Special). I remember a particular test drive after one of our "timing sessions" – we had stepped up the timing and then took the 'Stang out for a test drive. It was an unusual experience to feel like the car was "raring to go" after stopping for a traffic light – let's just say that the spark was coming a little early relative to the movement of the piston – so, we took that "pony" back to the "barn," i.e., workshop, for a few adjustments, and then she ran like a dream…ultimately, in the years to follow, with a rebuilt engine and a new paint job. I think we could all spend some time "in the workshop" adjusting our timing with God, the master creator and mechanic.

God, what can I do for you today…?
One day, Mother and I were reminiscing about restoring the Mustang. Then, Mother said, "like your Mustang, we can rebuild our thinking and start fresh. Just like restoring a classic car, we are never too old to start thinking God's way – you can always change your life and spend

time in His word and with His direction. We need to "live what the Bible says" to cover all phases and challenges in our lives. You are never too old to change; that is, a person can change his/her way of living, talking, doing for others, and lives will be changed for the better. They will get up each morning and ask 'What can I do today for God?'"

When we invite the Holy Spirit into our lives and ask that question, we may experience God's message of "Be still and know me." Other times, cognizance of a path or a person who needs us may come to mind. Steven Curtis Chapman's song entitled "Miracle of the Moment" [6] encourages us to recognize the significance of "right now" and make the most of the time we have. Pray about this today and relish the moments with family, friends, colleagues, new acquaintances, and "live in the moment" of new experiences. Even seemingly negative occurrences can become "teachable moments" and prepare us for the future. And, we may even laugh about the difficult situation one day… maybe.

∆∆∆∆∆ *Focus on the Lift* ∆∆∆∆∆

When we realize that our timing is not always God's timing… and that His timing is perfect, then we begin to recognize God's presence in our lives on a daily basis. He is there. Seek awareness of Him. Invite God and His son to be part of your life. Pray Ecclesiastes 3:1-8 with me:

There is an appointed time for everything. And there is a time for every event under heaven--
   A time to give birth and a time to die;
      A time to plant and a time to uproot what is planted.
   A time to kill and a time to heal;
      A time to tear down and a time to build up.
   A time to weep and a time to laugh;
      A time to mourn and a time to dance.
   A time to throw stones and a time to gather stones;
      A time to embrace and a time to shun embracing.

A time to search and a time to give up as lost;
 A time to keep and a time to throw away.
A time to tear apart and a time to sew together;
 A time to be silent and a time to speak.
A time to love and a time to hate;
 A time for war and a time for peace.

Let's schedule some time today to pray about God's timing of events within our lives. Ask Him to help you realize His presence in all of your experiences… in times of smiles and times of tears.

***

Moses parting the Red Sea… having unfaltering faith, following the path, and embracing God's grace…

Open your heart and experience stories of Moses leading the Israelites through hostile Egyptian territory. Feel as though you are on the journey with Moses. Feel the heat of the wilderness… breathe in and smell the salty sea air… and know that Moses is leading you with God's direction.

God Leads the People
Now when Pharaoh had let the people go, God did not lead them by the way of the land of the Philistines, even though it was near; for God said, "The people might change their minds when they see war, and return to Egypt."

Hence God led the people around by the way of the wilderness to the Red Sea; and the sons of Israel went up in martial array from the land of Egypt. [Exodus 13: 17-18]

The LORD was going before them in a pillar of cloud by day to lead them on the way, and in a pillar of fire by night to give them light, that they might travel by day and by night.

He did not take away the pillar of cloud by day, nor the pillar of fire by night, from before the people. [Exodus 13:21-22]

And, Exodus 14:

Pharaoh in Pursuit

Now the LORD spoke to Moses, saying,

"Tell the sons of Israel to turn back and camp before Pi-hahiroth, between Migdol and the sea; you shall camp in front of Baal-zephon, opposite it, by the sea.

"For Pharaoh will say of the sons of Israel, 'They are wandering aimlessly in the land; the wilderness has shut them in.' [Exodus 14:1-3]

The LORD hardened the heart of Pharaoh, king of Egypt, and he chased after the sons of Israel as the sons of Israel were going out boldly.

Then the Egyptians chased after them with all the horses and chariots of Pharaoh, his horsemen and his army, and they overtook them camping by the sea, beside Pi-hahiroth, in front of Baal-zephon.

As Pharaoh drew near, the sons of Israel looked, and behold, the Egyptians were marching after them, and they became very frightened; so the sons of Israel cried out to the LORD.

Then they said to Moses, "Is it because there were no graves in Egypt that you have taken us away to die in the wilderness? Why have you dealt with us in this way, bringing us out of Egypt?

"Is this not the word that we spoke to you in Egypt, saying, 'Leave us alone that we may serve the Egyptians'? For it would have been better for us to serve the Egyptians than to die in the wilderness."

The Sea Is Divided

But Moses said to the people, "Do not fear! Stand by and see the salvation of the LORD which He will accomplish for you today; for the Egyptians whom you have seen today, you will never see them again forever.

"The LORD will fight for you while you keep silent."

Then the LORD said to Moses, "Why are you crying out to Me? Tell the sons of Israel to go forward.

"As for you, lift up your staff and stretch out your hand over the sea and divide it, and the sons of Israel shall go through the midst of the sea on dry land.

"As for Me, behold, I will harden the hearts of the Egyptians so that they will go in after them; and I will be honored through Pharaoh and all his army, through his chariots and his horsemen.

"Then the Egyptians will know that I am the LORD, when I am honored through Pharaoh, through his chariots and his horsemen."

The angel of God, who had been going before the camp of Israel, moved and went behind them; and the pillar of cloud moved from before them and stood behind them.

"So it came between the camp of Egypt and the camp of Israel; and there was the cloud along with the darkness, yet it gave light at night. Thus the one did not come near the other all night.

Then Moses stretched out his hand over the sea; and the LORD swept the sea back by a strong east wind all night and turned the sea into dry land, so the waters were divided.

The sons of Israel went through the midst of the sea on the dry land, and the waters were like a wall to them on their right hand and on their left.

Then the Egyptians took up the pursuit, and all Pharaoh's horses, his chariots and his horsemen went in after them into the midst of the sea.

At the morning watch, the LORD looked down on the army of the Egyptians through the pillar of fire and cloud and brought the army of the Egyptians into confusion.

He caused their chariot wheels to swerve, and He made them drive with difficulty; so the Egyptians said, "Let us flee from Israel, for the LORD is fighting for them against the Egyptians."

Then the LORD said to Moses, "Stretch out your hand over the sea so that the waters may come back over the Egyptians, over their chariots and their horsemen."

So Moses stretched out his hand over the sea, and the sea returned to its normal state at daybreak, while the Egyptians were fleeing right into it; then the LORD overthrew the Egyptians in the midst of the sea.

The waters returned and covered the chariots and the horsemen, even Pharaoh's entire army that had gone into the sea after them; not even one of them remained.

But the sons of Israel walked on dry land through the midst of the sea, and the waters were like a wall to them on their right hand and on their left.

Thus the LORD saved Israel that day from the hand of the Egyptians, and Israel saw the Egyptians dead on the seashore.

When Israel saw the great power which the LORD had used against the Egyptians, the people feared the LORD, and they believed in the LORD and in His servant Moses. [Exodus 14:3-31]

Time to reflect…

Contemplate the verses you have just experienced. Moses had complete trust in God and God's timing. Thus, He called upon Moses and honed him into a leader. God is calling all of us right now to become servant-leaders. Jeremiah 17:7-8 reminds us "Blessed is the man who trusts in the LORD And whose trust is the LORD. For he will be like a tree planted by the water, That extends its roots by a stream And will not fear when the heat comes; But its leaves will be green, And it will not be anxious in a year of drought Nor cease to yield fruit."

On our t.v. show, *Golden Moments and Beyond*, Erin Campbell and I would frequently share stories of times when we attempted to "rely on our own understanding" and when plans went awry or outcomes seemed suboptimal, we came to realize that submitting the situation to God always yielded a more significant and sustainable result. Praise God that we have the opportunity to hand over control to Him. And, though we do not always know or understand His timing of events and situations in our lives, we do know that He is in control. Ask Jesus to carry you when you do not know where… or when… to take the next step. You can do this.

∆∆∆∆∆   *Focus on the Lift*   ∆∆∆∆∆

We are going to practice this idea of "letting go and letting God." Within the next twenty-four hours, all of us will experience a time when we try to control the outcome of something… a situation… a process… an interaction with others. So, let's consider our choices. We can either direct our efforts toward pushing our own ideas and agenda into the mix or step back to prayerfully contemplate how we can invite God into the decision-making process. Allow Him to direct our reactions and recommendations. Let's try this idea now. Pray with me: "Lord, please open our hearts and minds into awareness of Your leading presence. Help us to see Your planned outcomes and to more fully know You in the now, so that we can be Your feet and voice and hands. Please show us the way, Lord. Amen."

***

Now, it's time to begin fortifying ourselves as we continue to learn more about how reactions affect people in the now as well as on the horizon. Victim? Villain? Victor? Thinking about some titanium armor… like donning God's armor… let's continue this transformation into a stronger you… all for Him.

Chapter 4
Armor

ARMOR
by Albert Cloudy

There are those with everyday struggles
Easily hidden behind the smiles on their faces
By the constant reminder each day
They become used to the disadvantages
Toughens their soul to be immune
To hardships outside their problems
Makes them a stronger individual
More determined to fight for what they want
Their mind is like an armored truck
Keeps the enemy out and accepted in
Strong and willing to succeed
To let no one stop them from living out their dreams
Because of the strength and courage
You can be what you want to be.

©2016 Albert Cloudy. All rights reserved. Used with permission.

Armor of God…
Biblically, when we study Ephesians 6, we learn about something called the Armor of God. This armor reminds us that God can help us ward

off spiritual attacks… painful attacks such as the ones we all encounter through the harsh words and actions of other people. In this chapter, we will learn more about God's Armor. Ephesians 6 basically encourages us to "suit up in God's armor and prepare for change."

Each day, I pray protection over my family through donning the Armor of God (Ephesians 6). I prayerfully dress each of them in the helmet of salvation, breastplate of justice, belt of truth, footgear of zeal to spread God's word and gospel, and to carry the shield of faith and sword of the Word and Spirit. God is all about love and compassion. We are all called to share His love and compassion with others. It saddens me when I witness people acting harshly toward others… children and adults waste so much time judging each other. Each day, I ask God to help me not react to hurtful criticisms aimed at me, but rather to just let the words pass by. Next, I am praying to be able to smile while being judged. Working out at the gym is always good. The gym is a No Judgment Zone… it's all about the focus. Let's think about ways we can bring the gym mentality into our everyday lives. So, today, let's allow God to cover us with His armor… spiritual titanium… for protection from the "fire." So, hypothetically speaking, if one had the opportunity to cloak oneself in an armor composed of titanium, we would suppose that one could be adequately shielded from physical attack. Now, let's take this idea further.

Whenever in future wars the battle is fought,
armored troops will play the decisive role.
- Heinz Guderian

Protection through donning the Armor of God…

Let's pray together.

Lord, we ask you to dress us in Your Armor today. Help us to walk through the fires… climb over the walls… and crawl gracefully through the trenches that await us on this day. Clothe us in your helmet of salvation, your breastplate of justice, your belt of truth, your footgear of the zeal to share your Word and Gospel, and please help us to carry your shield of faith and the sword of your Word and Spirit. Thank you, Lord. Amen.

Again, we will don the Armor of God as we deepen our understanding of how strengthened relationships can be woven into our own *Titanium Transformation*.

In Paul's words:

"Finally, be strong in the Lord and in the strength of His might.

Put on the full armor of God, so that you will be able to stand firm against the schemes of the devil.

For our struggle is not against flesh and blood, but against the rulers, against the powers, against the world forces of this darkness, against the spiritual forces of wickedness in the heavenly places.

Therefore, take up the full armor of God, so that you will be able to resist in the evil day, and having done everything, to stand firm.

Stand firm therefore, HAVING GIRDED YOUR LOINS WITH TRUTH, and HAVING PUT ON THE BREASTPLATE OF RIGHTEOUSNESS,

and having shod YOUR FEET WITH THE PREPARATION OF THE GOSPEL OF PEACE;

in addition to all, taking up the shield of faith with which you will be able to extinguish all the flaming arrows of)the evil one.

And take THE HELMET OF SALVATION, and the sword of the Spirit, which is the word of God.

With all prayer and petition pray at all times in the Spirit, and with this in view, be on the alert with all perseverance and petition for all the saints,

and pray on my behalf, that utterance may be given to me in the opening of my mouth, to make known with boldness the mystery of the gospel,

for which I am an ambassador in chains; that in proclaiming it I may speak boldly, as I ought to speak.

But that you also may know about my circumstances, how I am doing, Tychicus, the beloved brother and faithful minister in the Lord, will make everything known to you.

I have sent him to you for this very purpose, so that you may know about us, and that he may comfort your hearts.

Peace be to the brethren, and love with faith, from God the Father and the Lord Jesus Christ.

Grace be with all those who love our Lord Jesus Christ with incorruptible love." [Ephesians 6:10-24]

So, Paul calls us into the battle to colonize God's kingdom through spreading the teachings of the gospel… the story of Jesus' time here on earth and the lessons he spoke straight from His Father. He tells us to "pray at all times in the Spirit" and also to pray for clarity of the spoken word while preaching "with boldness the mystery of the gospel." Paul is talking about communicating effectively, which is imperative for all of us when we are interacting with others… delivering a message… engaging in dialogue. When we are trying to build and strengthen relationships, effective communication is so very important.

When others don't understand…words can hurt…
This morning, the words from others around me were so inspiring… was feeling uplifted… high on life. Then, this afternoon, the words from

these same people were mean-spirited. Those who know me recognize that I have many physical scars from a car wreck. But, hurtful language can leave emotional scars which are not always so obvious to others. While listening this time though, I was praying that God would help me interpret the harshness of the remarks that were being poured upon me - was there some spiritually significant purpose? Yes… actually it is a calling… a reach out to all who are struggling with being bullied. No, bullying behavior does not end when you graduate from school. Adults engage in malicious word-shaking as well. The Bible instructs us to use the spoken word to teach, encourage, support, empathize with, and love others. James 1:19 teaches us to be quick to listen… slow to speak… and slow to anger. Then, add into the mix the notion of trying to pray for interpretation while facing a verbal firing squad. Spiritual multitasking? In a way… yes. Sometimes, life can feel like a mine field where we do not know what will happen with each step we take. We all have people in our lives who cause us to doubt ourselves and not to be cliché, but they make us feel like we are walking on egg shells when in their presence because those people slam us with harsh words no matter what we say or do. Words can hurt and words can heal. Let's think about what Romans 5:1-5 shares with us about feeling the Holy Spirit's presence in the midst of difficult situations:

Therefore, having been justified by faith, we have peace with God through our Lord Jesus Christ, through whom also we have obtained our introduction by faith into this grace in which we stand; and we exult in hope of the glory of God. And not only this, but we also exult in our tribulations, knowing that tribulation brings about perseverance; and perseverance, proven character; and proven character, hope; and hope does not disappoint, because the love of God has been poured out within our hearts through the Holy Spirit who was given to us. [Romans 5:1-5]

Words can hurt and words can heal…
So, how do we gather the needed strength and knowledge to mitigate our own and others' daily struggles? Bullying is one of those struggles

which many innocent children must face every day. Recently, I had the opportunity to talk with Christine Schmidt, co-founder of an organization called I.A.L.O.L. which stands for It's All Love Only Love. Christine's story is one of great pain, yet she wants to share her experience to help prevent others from a tragedy that we are hearing more and more about in the news and in our own communities: adolescent suicide. Christine's daughter, Morgan, took her own life one spring day in 2014. Morgan was being bullied by her peers at school. Some students were jealous of her achievements, and as so many of us know, jealousy is often at the root of cruelty. Before Morgan died, there were some dramatic and hurtful situations where "friends" would intentionally exclude her from their activities and then text pictures of their gatherings to Morgan in order to hurt her feelings. There is nothing new about drama and mean behavior among young girls… but with today's technology and ever increasing data transfer speeds, one could say that it is easier and quicker to bring about emotional pain. Morgan was twelve years old when she took her last breath. I asked Christine if there were any signs leading up to her daughter's suicide. Was there any indication that she was having suicidal thoughts? Her reply: "Yes. Actually there were signs, but in order to have had a chance of preventing what was about to happen, it would have required communication between Morgan's friends, family, and school leaders. If we had only talked with each other about some unusual behaviors which Morgan was displaying, she might be alive today." Christine goes on to tell me about the things Morgan was doing at home and at school that were not typical for her, such as: at home, she was suddenly having extreme difficulty sleeping at night and then she began to clean out her closet and room – giving items to family members and charities. At school, she had been cleaning out her locker and giving mementos like photographs and souvenirs to friends. Remember, at this time it was spring. School was still in full session. Also, while at school, she was going to the nurse's office about every other day complaining of stomachaches and headaches while telling the nurse she just wanted to go home. Sometimes the school nurse would call Christine and sometimes she would send Morgan back to class since she did not have a fever or outwardly visible signs of illness.

Now, Christine is seeking opportunities to bring her I.A.L.O.L. programs into schools where she and her team can educate others about how and why communication with our children can be life-giving… and ultimately life-saving. She talks with parents and school leaders about sharing the responsibility for teaching children: kindness, compassion, validation, emphasis, and affirmation. She is asking adults to engage in open dialogue with children and students about how being kind can improve the child's own confidence and self-esteem, not to mention that of the recipients of kind acts. "Pay it forward," Christine says. She shares stories of compassion for others and ways that we can validate others' feelings. For example, if your child or student tells you that he/she is being bullied, Christine says that instead of telling him/her to just ignore it and it will go away, to instead validate their feelings by asking them about the situation and about their feelings. She further recommends that we place the correct emphasis on the situation, as in whether an adult should intervene. And, affirming our child's positive behaviors and achievements – no matter the size – is key to helping build his/her confidence and self-esteem. Christine says that she aims to "change the hearts of children… both present and future." She talks about peers' use of technology when bullying her daughter, Morgan. "But," she says, "technology can be used for promoting kindness. It's the message that's being communicated… not the method of communication that's the problem."

Here's another question: What is the likelihood that "bullies" are being bullied in some manner in their own lives? Could they be mirroring behavior that they are seeing at home or in school? And, realize that many of us have a stereotypical image of what a "bully" looks like, possibly from cartoons and television shows, or maybe from our own childhood experiences. Know this though – bullies appear in many forms and sizes… even petite pretty schoolgirls can become bullies unless they learn how to be kind to their peers.

The Schmidt family members are firm in their spiritual beliefs and recognize that God is giving them His grace and strength to help other people avoid experiencing the loss of a loved one from suicide. "It's all love... only love," Morgan liked to say. Christine adds, "God is calling His army to help save children's lives. Come join us. Because you know, It's All Love Only Love."

Let your speech always be with grace, as though seasoned with salt, so that you will know how you should respond to each person. [Colossians 4:6]

∆∆∆∆∆   Focus on the Lift   ∆∆∆∆∆

Today, let's pray about how to speak kind words to others around us. Let's "Speak Life"[1] as Toby Mac sings. Ask God to give you the words.

***

There is an unwritten rule at the gym. The gym is a "no judgment zone" where you focus on your own workout without criticizing how people look or how they are exercising. Hmmmmm... what if we apply this unwritten rule to life and the way we interact with other people... like we are instructed in Luke 6:31 "Treat others the same way you want them to treat you." And, then let's consider the art of effective and encouraging communication. Psalm 95 teaches us to listen for God's voice and be open to uplifting conversation.

A true voyage of discovery does not consist of seeking new landscapes but rather of seeing with new eyes.- Marcel Proust

∆∆∆∆∆   Focus on the Lift   ∆∆∆∆∆

So, it's been a long day... but good day... you agree? Now we are here quietly reflecting on the day's experiences... some to smile about... some to pray about... some to ponder... some to celebrate. You know... there is a point in each of our own lives where we recognize the value of perseverance... patience... and playfulness... cool. We need to persevere toward our goals while patiently respecting the time it takes to get there. And, knowing that if we can't laugh a little along the way we are definitely taking ourselves too seriously and others will pass us by. Soooooooooo... what made you smile today? What caused you to persevere even harder? What reminded you that patience is a virtue? What made you feel blessed? Let's begin and finish each day with a joyful heart and the passion to make a life changing difference... in ourselves... in others... in this world...yes... Come on... Let's Do This.

Here's something that made me smile today when I saw it: J35US (on a Florida license plate)

***

Remember the Invitation…
As we always have the opportunity to enjoy some High Tea with the Trinity, let's read the following scripture in Proverbs 9 and ask God to help us understand the meaning of His message to us.

Proverbs 9…
Wisdom's Invitation
    Wisdom has built her house,
        She has hewn out her seven pillars;
    She has prepared her food, she has mixed her wine;
        She has also set her table;
    She has sent out her maidens, she calls
        From the tops of the heights of the city:
    "Whoever is naive, let him turn in here!"
        To him who lacks understanding she says,
    "Come, eat of my food
        And drink of the wine I have mixed.
    "Forsake your folly and live,
        And proceed in the way of understanding."
    He who corrects a scoffer gets dishonor for himself,

    And he who reproves a wicked man gets insults for himself.
Do not reprove a scoffer, or he will hate you,
    Reprove a wise man and he will love you.
Give instruction to a wise man and he will be still wiser,
    Teach a righteous man and he will increase his learning.
The fear of the LORD is the beginning of wisdom,
    And the knowledge of the Holy One is understanding.
For by me your days will be multiplied,
    And years of life will be added to you. [Proverbs 9:1-18]

Message: We are being called into Communion…to be Reconciled with our Brothers and Sisters everywhere… knowing that God brings us Redemption… Forgiveness… Inheritance… Salvation… Hope… Compassion… and Strength. Now is the time for reconciliation and ending the enmity in communities across the world.

Ever wonder why…
by Ginny Frings

As the sun shines down
Upon the many souls in this town
Who knows where this day will go
As we determinably race to and fro
To get the job done or so we think
When really there is a higher purpose to our lives
Sitting here on the brink
Of a time when… and a place where
People who do not know us will stop and stare
And ask why the rounds we keep making
While the world around us seems to be quaking
All the bullying and fighting needs to stop right now
No one appears to have the answer how
Maybe we all need to look up from our task
And just take the time to ask
No matter our color or our race

Each one of us has a face…
And a voice…
It's a choice…
To come together or not
To help heal this world or let it rot
Let's choose the first
And work together to quench this thirst
For reconciliation, peace, and love
All are a gift from above
We are being called to walk hand in hand
Woman, child, and man
To cross the great divide that is tearing this country apart
Now is the time to answer the call with an open heart
And to look to the sky…
Ever wonder why?

©2016 Ginny W. Frings. All rights reserved. Use only with written permission.

Leaders for God within and among us…
As we gather the strength to journey through these trials we all are facing in our lives, oftentimes we will feel the urge to reach out to others to glean leadership during our times of distress. Other times, God may have us use our experiences to help lead someone else successfully through their predicament. Think about the scene in the Bible where Jesus was questioning Simon about his love. As Simon responded favorably to each inquiry, Jesus gave him a directive. We are all being called to follow these same directives – to lead and to love.

"So when they had finished breakfast, Jesus said to Simon Peter, "Simon, son of John, do you love Me more than these?" He said to Him, "Yes, Lord; You know that I love You " He said to him, "Tend My lambs." He said to him again a second time, "Simon, son of John, do you love Me?" He said to Him, "Yes, Lord; You know that I love You." He said to him, "Shepherd My sheep." He said to him the third time, "Simon, son of John, do you love Me?" Peter was grieved because He said to him the third time, "Do you love Me?" And he said to Him, "Lord, You know all things; You know that I love You " Jesus said to him, "Tend My sheep." [John 21:15-17]

And, we are encouraged and commanded to love one another…

"Love is patient, love is kind and is not jealous; love does not brag and is not arrogant, does not act unbecomingly; it does not seek its own, is not provoked, does not take into account a wrong suffered, does not rejoice in unrighteousness, but rejoices with the truth; bears all things, believes all things, hopes all things, endures all things." [1Corinthians 13:4-7]

Do you know someone like Jack?…
As we are learning how to lead and love others unconditionally, as directed through Scripture, we experience our own changes and challenges… actual or perceived… each day of our lives. Sometimes… often times even… we may allow these periods of difficulty to interfere with relationships in multiple areas of our lives. It is sad when that happens, but we all know how it feels when we project our frustration onto someone else. How can we learn to embrace rather than become stressed over the changes? Distress is not a productive emotion. If we ask God to help us work through the situation, He will illuminate our lives – sometimes the *brightest* of ideas come to mind on the seemingly *darkest* of days. God wants us to witness and live with a faithful and positive outlook. Here is a true story about someone who does that each day. Jack Smith, an officer with the Xavier University Campus Police Department, oversees the check-in gate at the entrance to one of the faculty parking areas at Xavier University in Cincinnati, Ohio. His faith and optimistic outlook are inspiring.

Jack's gate is known on campus as "The Positive Gate" because he can help you see the positive side of practically any situation which you are working to endure. No matter what your mood, the weather, current events in the world, or "busy-ness" of your schedule for the day is, Jack's pleasant greeting, sense of humor, and insights into life's lessons will encourage and put you in the right frame of mind to go about your work day with peace of mind. He is genuinely interested in what you perceive to be your challenges, and then he helps you know that those perceived challenges could more likely become uncovered opportunities. Next, he will talk with you for a few minutes to plant a seed of inspiration. There have been days where it seemed like it was the end of the road for me… doors had closed on opportunities… situations that had once appeared to be on the right track went sideways… and not knowing which way to turn… when driving to work and deciding to drive through "The Positive Gate" and listen to Jack's positive comments have always made a tremendous difference. Many faculty, students, and staff at Xavier have commented on Jack's encouragement and commitment to doing God's work while he is here on earth. And, be assured that the next time you see Jack on campus and he asks you how things are going… and you tell him about the opportunities that have come about in your life and how you are pursuing God's direction… Jack will say, "Didn't we discuss this? And, didn't I tell you that everything would work out?" Jack is a leader for God. Thank you, Jack, for keeping "The Positive Gate" and for helping us to keep the faith.

Who… What… Where…
Just like Jack, we are all being called to be stewards. In Luke 16:13, we are told that we cannot serve two masters. Our love and devotion placed with God will equip us to become successful stewards of each other and of the resources with which God has gifted us. We need to remember this idea when situations arise which could foible our spiritual walk or cause us to follow someone who is trying to lead us astray. As we continue to *Focus on the Lift* in this chapter, think about this…

What is your next step on your personal journey?

Ginny W. Frings, Ph.D.

∆∆∆∆∆   *Focus on the Lift*   ∆∆∆∆∆

We all experience change. Circumstances in our lives can lead us to question why we are on a particular path and why challenges sometimes seem like roadblocks. Recently, my husband, Michael, and I were discussing ways to approach a potentially difficult situation where people's personalities and biases were delaying the implementation of a rather simple solution to the problem. As we were discussing which steps to take and how to embrace the situation, he said to me: "You have to know who you are, what you are, and where you are." And then I said, "before you can pursue the path God has planned for you." He said, "Exactly!" Step back for a moment of quiet reflection and dialogue with God over the problem and workable solution(s). Talk with God about who, what, and where you are. He will share insights into your path and answers to your questions.

I think we all have questions, especially during times of change. What changes are you facing right now? Does it seem like intended solutions are faltering? Are doors closing? Is there a fog obscuring your view of the horizon? We are learning to let God clear the fog, shed His light, and share His timing.

Before we continue learning about God's leading in our lives, let's take some time to pray about who, what, and where we are. In a notebook, write the following four column headings at the tops of seven different pages:

<u>Date   Who   What   Where</u>

Then, for the next seven days, fill in the columns by writing down with whom you spoke, what you discussed, and where you had the conversation – including phone calls, webcasts, e-mails, and texts!

Then, after seven days, reflect on your recorded interactions. Were there some difficult discussions? Why? Invite God to pull up a chair and sit beside you right now. Ask Him to guide your speech and help you to see the path more clearly.

God sent His Son, Jesus, to come live among us on earth. His presence can still be felt and seen. We just need to clear away some of the stuff that's fogging our view of God within our daily lives.

***

High Fives Happening Here…
One sunny Sunday afternoon, we took the children to a local amusement park and had fun riding the rides and playing games. Toward the end of the day, as the sun was setting, my daughter and I noticed a young gentleman who was wearing a white t-shirt, walking along, and happily giving people "high fives" left and right. Then, we saw the front of his t-shirt and his smiling face. His t-shirt read: "Get Your Free High Fives Here!" in bright fluorescent green letters. What a wonderful idea… making people smile on a Sunday evening, a time when many people are thinking about the upcoming week's deadlines and going to work the next day, and they are just trying to make the most of those final weekend moments. We should all give more "high fives" each day… even for achievements that may seem trivial to us… think about how recognizing someone's effort, though maybe small, will encourage that person to persevere. Getting a "high five" in one setting of that person's life can help them work through difficulties in other areas of their lives. We do not know how far reaching a little encouragement can go. We only know how it feels to travel our own road. A few months after that day in the amusement park, we saw a car license plate that read: AHI52U. Now, that's a cool reminder…

△△△△△ ***Focus on the Lift*** △△△△△

This exercise involves thinking of others. The Commandment to "love one another " includes encouraging each other. Let's live this Commandment today: at least five times today, give someone words of encouragement, either spoken, written, or communicated in some way that is meaningful to the other person - could even be a real "high five" and a smile! When the other person smiles back at you, how does that make you feel? Pretty good, huh? When we show Christ's love to others, it comes back to us multiplied. After each "sharing of a high five" experience, write a few lines about the interaction – who, scenario, how they reacted, and how it made you feel.

***

Now, let's relax with Jesus…

Jesus Stills the Sea

On that day, when evening came, He said to them, "Let us go over to the other side."

Leaving the crowd, they took Him along with them in the boat, just as He was; and other boats were with Him.

And there arose a fierce gale of wind, and the waves were breaking over the boat so much that the boat was already filling up.

Jesus Himself was in the stern, asleep on the cushion; and they woke Him and said to Him, "Teacher, do You not care that we are perishing?"

And He got up and rebuked the wind and said to the sea, "Hush, be still." And the wind died down and it became perfectly calm.

And He said to them, "Why are you afraid? Do you still have no faith?"

They became very much afraid and said to one another, "Who then is this, that even the wind and the sea obey Him?" [Mark 4:35-41]

In this scriptural passage, we experience the questioning of the new disciples, the power of God working through Jesus, and God's question to us: "Why are you so afraid?" Again, why are you so afraid? What are you afraid of? The circumstances of our world in transition can cause us to be "on edge" and feel as though we are standing on the plank… trying not to rock the boat and perish in the storm. As the winds blow and the water rises, ask God to carry you and guide your travels through life. Remember, Jeremiah 10:23 "I know, O LORD, that a man's way is not in himself, Nor is it in a man who walks to direct his steps."

God will direct your step. Just ask Him.

The question…
Now, we can build upon our foundation for learning to recognize God's presence in our lives each day. Let's do this by adding "change" analysis to this foundation. Unexpected circumstances, e.g., like the storm in the above story, and changes occur every day. How often do we hear the phrase, "not sure which way the wind is blowing" in reference to someone's changing attitude or reactions to problems in a project plan? What do we do when the winds of life blow? Do we retreat? Build a wall and wait for the "wind," i.e., change, to stop blowing and leave us alone? Or do we build a "windmill" and use the situation as a tool for witnessing to the strength and power of God the Almighty? Let's pray about this question: In times of strife, we can think "WWJD" - i.e., ask ourselves what would Jesus do if He were in my shoes? Like Steven Curtis Chapman sings in his song "The Change"[2] when he asks about when people see a person with a WWJD bumper sticker or bracelet, do they see that person as a true follower of God and a witness to His grace and glory… do they see "the difference"… "the change"… "the witness" in that person's life and desire to have God's direction in their own lives? Or, do they see someone talking one way and acting in another less favorable manner? In Hebrews 12:1, we are told that we are operating every day "in a cloud of witnesses" and people are watching us as we pursue our path of life. Are we exemplifying the search for the path we say we are seeking, i.e., are we "walking the walk" and "talking the talk"? Though cliché in nomenclature, these are deep questions that we need to answer on our road to salvation. When you do not know

which way to go, ask Jesus what He would do and He will answer you. During our own waves of change and uncertainty, many people have these questions:

- How do we embrace the situation with anticipation and the drive to succeed?
- How can we transform challenges into victories?
- How can we best manage unexpected opportunities?

What's different?...
Have you ever found yourself commenting that someone has "changed" but you are not sure how? Different hair style? Maybe they have lost weight? Is there a new sense of calmness that now emanates from this person? What's different about him or her? I have always enjoyed working the "what's wrong with this picture" and "how many differences can you find" puzzles – as a child and even now! I am continually seeking to hone a keener sense of awareness. Think about how Mary felt when she came upon the empty tomb. And, how Jesus' followers must have felt when they learned that the tomb was empty, and then they witnessed His presence brought through resurrection. Was that a period of change in their lives… and Jesus' life? Indeed, it was.

The equation… replacing the fear…
Students in my classes at the university are unsure of what the future holds… career-wise, economically, politically, and environmentally. Many of us possess those same concerns while we work through the "school of life" every day. How do we arise each day in anticipation of the "changes" we are going to experience, rather than hesitancy about the "challenges" that may come our way? These questions have been in my heart and on my mind since I began writing *U R Titanium*. We are all seeking who we are meant to be – reminds me of the message in Michael W. Smith's song "Rise."[3]

How do we define "challenges"? Why do people tend to view working through a solution to a "challenge" as more difficult than surviving a "change"? Think about this equation:

CHANGE = CHALLENGE − LLE

LLE = **L**ife **L**earning **E**xperiences that help us to see the need for God's direction in our lives and transform a seemingly grandiose challenge into a manageable change that we, with God's help, feel that we can handle.

In this book, we are learning how to transform a challenge into a more positive change… sometimes the transformation requires shifting some priorities or automating some processes, i.e., removing some letters (c-h-a-l-l-e-n-g-e into c-h-a-n-g-e). And, sometimes we will need to work on a deeper level, beginning with identifying why we perceive life the way we do. In *Navigate with God*[4], we looked internally at our prayer lives, and then honed our skills of awareness of God's presence in our lives, woven together with the threads of true stories about the wonderment of God's grace, scriptural reflections, and opportunities to dialogue with God and His Son. As we continue on our journey to nearness and serenity in a life with our Lord and savior, Jesus Christ, let's take some time to talk with God about our travels and planned destination.

∆ ∆ ∆ ∆ *Focus on the Lift* ∆ ∆ ∆ ∆

Approach this exercise of life transformation by relaxing in prayer with Jesus, and then contemplating your life experiences. First, think about your accomplishments… could be educational… familial… occupational… relational… spiritual… recreational… philanthropical… personal. Next, thank God for guiding you through your accomplishments. Then, think about the challenges are you facing - are they short-term or long-term? Write down your accomplishments. Again, thank God for His blessings. Then, write down the challenges in your life. Pray for direction. Do you feel like you are on a "solo flight"? Know that you are not. God is with you. What ideas come to mind? Write those down. You may not have realized it at the time, but your accomplishments are "Life Learning Experiences" that have been preparing you to meet your current challenges, and thus, providing you with insights on how to navigate change in your world. Pray about this idea and ask God for revelation. Invite Jesus into your heart and ask to be filled with the Holy Spirit. Think about Jesus' road… and the cross He had to bear. His life experiences are still teaching us through scripture and His presence in our lives. Let's ask Jesus to help us understand as we prepare to accept God's invitation.

There is an invitation waiting in your spiritual mailbox. Write your acceptance to God's invitation to join Him and His Son for an afternoon of high tea that will last a lifetime. The Holy Spirit is nudging you.. you get that feeling… yes?

***

Jesus among His Disciples
So when it was evening on that day, the first day of the week, and when the doors were shut where the disciples were, for fear of the Jews, Jesus came and stood in their midst and said to them, "Peace be with you."

And when He had said this, He showed them both His hands and His side The disciples then rejoiced when they saw the Lord.

So Jesus said to them again, "Peace be with you; as the Father has sent Me, I also send you."

And when He had said this, He breathed on them and said to them, "Receive the Holy Spirit. [John 20:19-22]

Prayerfully ask right now to have the Holy Spirit breathed into you. Experience the weight of the world being lifted from your shoulders… and a rush of calmness flowing within you. You need not worry. 1Peter 5:6-7 tells us "Therefore humble yourselves under the mighty hand of God, that He may exalt you at the proper time, casting all your anxiety on Him, because He cares for you."

Treasuring life while being still and knowing God is here…
"…Store up for yourselves treasures in heaven, where neither moth nor rust destroys, and where thieves do not break in or steal; for where your treasure is, there your heart will be also." [Matthew 6:20-21]

Each morning begins a new day. I like to walk along the beach to see what treasures God is sharing with me this day. Along the shore, there are beautiful shells mixed with patches of seaweed brought into shore with the waves, and often there are pieces of debris discarded into nature by humans. If we will ask God, He will help us sort through and recycle the rubbish in our lives and focus on the heavenly treasures He has waiting for us. He will even help us see the beauty beyond the façade. For example, think of multiple uses for seaweed… even as a delicacy in spring rolls! While standing at the shoreline with the cool morning tide washing over my toes, I look out to the horizon and a song comes to mind, Steven Curtis' Chapman's "Treasure Island." [5] His lyrics remind me that we need to give our concerns to God and take time to seek the treasure in God's word each day. We can focus on Him to see what He provides while sustaining us through life's breakers.

Let's continue our walk along the beach… oh, there it is… a glistening white sand dollar tucked under the sand with just an edge showing. I absolutely love sand dollars. They are like treasures of the sea - often hidden. One morning, while swimming along the shore in Destin, Florida, I came across a bed of live sand dollars. They were brown in color and their cilia where working to trap plankton particles as the tide flowed over their home. There is a Christian legend of sand dollars where the beautiful white shell looks to be etched with a cross and inside there are smaller shells resembling white doves. It was interesting to observe the living sand dollars nestled safely on the sandy floor as they were peacefully awaiting the next wave to bring with it food for their sustenance and growth.

In 2Corinthians 4:6-8, we learn that we have God's treasures within us:

"For God, who said, "Light shall shine out of darkness," is the One who has shone in our hearts to give the Light of the knowledge of the glory of God in the face of Christ. But we have this treasure in earthen vessels, so that the surpassing greatness of the power will be of God and not from ourselves; *we are* afflicted in every way, but not crushed; perplexed, but not despairing;"

In a way, we are like the treasured sand dollar. Think about it. What outward signs do we share with others to be examples of the caring humanity that God brought to the earth through Christ, His Son? Like using our hands to help others? Lending a listening ear? Sharing the voice of truth? Using our feet to walk the journey of compassion to the aid of others in this world? And further, what about our "white doves" on the inside? Do we carry Christ within us… within our own earthen vessels… to share with others?

When we feel weary, it can be difficult to be a "sand dollar treasure" for others… even those closest to us. Sometimes we need to be shattered and rebuilt before we can recognize and effectively share the treasure which God has placed within us. And so the story begins…

The façade… all shiny and bright…
In the year 2000, I was a new mom of baby twins and working at my first job as a doctorate level educator. With our recent move to a new town with my husband's job, coupled with my new responsibilities at home and work, I was personally wielding a double type A personality mixed with the trait of extreme perfectionism. I was tired… physically, mentally, emotionally, and spiritually. Each day, I was trying to recall how it had once felt to walk with Jesus and dialogue with Him about life's decisions, but I was so fatigued with all the demands on my time. With a new job, new house, new babies, and a red convertible… everyone around us thought I had it all together! That was most definitely not the case. If only they could have seen the spiritual turmoil going on inside of me! Looking back, it felt as though I was battling God. The Holy Spirit was trying to communicate with me, but I had shut off my senses

to spiritual leadings. I was no longer dialoguing with God. All I was concerned about was trying to maintain my own spirit of perfectionism and a blissful façade. It was so draining to try to keep up the appearance that everything was fine, that even a glimmer of latent memories could not renew my walk with Him. Why did I feel compelled at that time in my life to even try to make everything look OK? I was trying to be humanly strong, but I was spiritually weak and headed for what felt like a spiritual calamity, and I did not know which way to turn to get off that road. I am reminded of the Michael W. Smith song entitled "Breathe in Me" [6] where he asks to receive the breath of the Holy Spirit and be renewed. I, too, felt "so dead within" at that time in my life.

One night in May of 2000, I dreamt that I was the survivor of a head-on car collision. Upon awakening, I was trying to pray for interpretation of the dream… nightmarish in experiencing the collision… miraculous in how in the dream I walked away unscathed and then receiving the gift of seeing the many friends and family members who appeared in that dream. I really did not think too much more about it and just returned to the details of daily life. God's miracles were all around me. It was as if I was behind a veil and could not see that reality.

Isaiah 41:20 tells us: That they may see and recognize,
And consider and gain insight as well,
That the hand of the Lord has done this,
And the Holy One of Israel has created it.

The Crash…When Life Shatters…

Then, my husband and I both received upwardly mobile job opportunities in another city. So, we put the house on the market; my husband moved into temporary housing in the new city until we could join him; and we decided that the babies and I should take a short trip to Alabama to visit family before the household move that summer. We did just that and enjoyed a nice visit. Then, something happened that would forever change our lives. On the way back home to Virginia, right outside Knoxville, Tennessee, another driver was driving the wrong way on the interstate. The other driver was trying to evade capture by police by purposefully going the wrong way and crashed head-on into our car. (I learned later while talking with the Sheriff, that the other driver survived the crash and was fine – and that she stated she had intended to end her life that night by crashing into another car). In the conversation with the Sheriff, my questions were answered … except for one … "Why me?" And, only God would answer that question in due time.

"But we have this treasure in earthen vessels, so that the surpassing greatness of the power will be of God and not from ourselves; *we are* afflicted in every way, but not crushed; perplexed, but not despairing; persecuted, but not forsaken; struck down, but not destroyed; always carrying about in the body the dying of Jesus, so that the life of Jesus also may be manifested in our body. For we who live are constantly being delivered over to death for Jesus' sake, so that the life of Jesus also may be manifested in our mortal flesh. So death works in us, but life in you." (2Corinthians 4:7-12)

It felt as though my earthen vessel had been crushed. Some people who visited me in the hospital said that I was barely recognizable due to the trauma my body had endured.

Gathering the pieces…

Our baby twins survived (and since I have worked to help educate others on the importance of child passenger safety). The paramedics extracted me from the car (I was told later that it took them 1 ½ hours to get me out of the car and that the babies miraculously slept through that) and then they air-ambulanced me to UT-Knoxville Medical Center. The doctors on call pronounced my injuries. In addition to a head injury, both of my legs and my left arm were broken, along with a broken pelvis, broken right foot, and internal bleeding. In their opinion, I was at death's door. But, for some reason they started rebuilding me.

They told my husband that I would not live, but if by some miracle I did regain consciousness, I would never walk again and because of my head injury, I would be a vegetable. After twenty-two pints of blood were administered, my husband said that he lost count of how many additional pints were needed during the initial emergency surgeries. Philippians 4:13 says "I can do all things through Him who strengthens me."

The trauma surgeons on call (who had already been in surgery for twelve straight hours that day) rebuilt me with stainless steel parts … metal rods, plates, and screws (and still today, I set off those metal detectors in the airports every time!) The scenario reminds me of the story of Humpty Dumpty. Unlike Humpty Dumpty, with all of the king's horses and all of the king's men, thank goodness all of the doctors with God's help *could* put me back together, again! As scripture says, "For He will command His angels concerning you to guard you in all your ways." [Psalm 91:11]

Thoughts on repairs…like chinks in my physical armor…
After seven days on a ventilator, I awoke in Trauma ICU with two questions on my mind: "What happened?" and "Where are my babies?" It was a living nightmare waiting to hear the answers. The nurses and doctors began to tell me the story with the added prognosis for my life: "Ginny, you are awake now. But, you will never walk or regain use of your left arm, again." At that point, I had survived five of the twelve orthopedic surgeries that I would endure during the next six years. While existing in a wheelchair and having physical therapy every day, many people encouraged me to speak and write about my journey to recovery and spiritual growth. My father-in-law said, "Ginny, you have been through a mess – now you have a message. You have been through a test and now you have a testimony." I felt like a child reaching for my Father's hand so I could learn how to walk, again. In Matthew 19:26 we hear: "And looking at them Jesus said to them, 'With people this is impossible, but with God all things are possible.'"

Further, we need to remember: "For I am convinced that neither death, nor life, nor angels, nor principalities, nor things present, nor things to come, nor powers, nor height, nor depth, nor any other created thing, will be able to separate us from the love of God, which is in Christ Jesus our Lord." (Romans 8:38-39)

∆ ∆ ∆ ∆ ∆ *Focus on the Lift* ∆ ∆ ∆ ∆ ∆

The scripture that we just read, Romans 8:38-39, teaches us that nothing can separate us from God. Yes, true, but we often allow ourselves to feel as though we are separated from Him. Why do we do this? What types of situations and relationships in your life cause you to feel isolated from Christ's love? In reality, He is walking beside you right in this minute and He is willing to carry you when you ask Him to do so. Pray with me now as we lift up all that you feel is keeping you from God's engagement within your life. Let's do this. Here. Now.

***

Get ready to explore ways that we can take the next steps into recognizing and realizing God's loving and leading presence, which exists all around us.

Chapter 5

∞∞∞∞∞∞∞∞ Next... Step... ∞∞∞∞∞∞∞∞

NEXT
by Albert Cloudy

What's wanted in life is not the impossible
Clear that path. There is nothing stopping you
Where you are now can always go further
The next move on the board game
Looking back to see from which you came
Know what you want plan to get it
The goals you want to reach
Strive and achieve it
No matter how far you get
There's always time to climb and figure out what is next
Next is something you should already know
That it's your life that it's not a joke
So think real hard how you'll be your best
Ask yourself now what is next?

©2016 Albert Cloudy. All rights reserved. Used with permission.

Question: *Since surviving a near-death experience, I continue to ask God: "What should I do next?"*

Answer: The next step is to <u>let God help us with the heavy lifting in our lives.</u>

ΔΔΔΔΔ   *Focus on the Lift*   ΔΔΔΔΔ

Before we continue with the spiritual building process, i.e., our *Titanium Transformation*, let's think about this truth. God speaks to us every day. He shares His wisdom and insights with us. Are we listening? What about those great ideas that suddenly come to mind and will not disappear? The nudges to step out of our comfort zones? Intuition about the outcome of a certain project? Could God be trying to get your attention? He wants to help you reach for and achieve the goals on your life path. He will make your daily "workouts" purposeful – intellectually, spiritually, and physically! Do you feel like you are progressing toward your goals... taking the next step... focusing on the lift? Think about your own motivation... inspiration... and determination. You can go get those goals! Come on... Let's Do This.

"The LORD will fight for you while you keep silent." (Exodus 14:14) *Remember, the letters* in S-I-L-E-N-T *spell* L-I-S-T-E-N.

Prayerfully, ask Jesus to help make you more aware of this idea that is so true: "The creation of a thousand forests are in one acorn." Ralph Waldo Emerson

There is one God... one Body of Christ... but the many people on earth are the many members of the Body of Christ.

***

Still on the road to recovery and the journey continues... the next step?
A month later, we are still at UT Medical Center in Knoxville, Tennessee. Our house is still on the market in Lynchburg, Virginia. We have not looked at houses in Richmond, Virginia. My car wreck happened after my husband had been working at his new job in Richmond for two

weeks. After the coma, surviving six of the twelve surgeries that will be required for my recovery during the following six years, unexpectedly awakening, and existing in the Tennessee hospital for over a month, the doctors then tell us that I need to be moved to a rehabilitation hospital to give me the best chance of recovering some, if any, function of my three non-functioning limbs (both legs and my left arm and hand). My husband begins checking into the programs available in the Knoxville area, Lynchburg, and Richmond rehabilitation hospitals. There is a reputable rehab facility in Knoxville, but they would not take me because I have too many injuries – one too many limbs are not functioning for their minimum requirements on initial mobility. Lynchburg does not have the facilities necessary for my treatment. Next, he calls Sheltering Arms Hospital in Mechanicsville, Virginia (suburb of Richmond), and they tell him to have me air-ambulanced to their location. Sheltering Arms is an answer to prayer. We would be able to get the whole family together in one city. Friends and family came to help take care of the babies while I lived at the rehabilitation hospital and my husband went back to work. Question that is on our minds at this point: Will I ever walk, or use my left arm and hand, again?

Keeping the faith…

As these questions continued to run through my mind each day, my cousin, Maria, kept reminding me of these words:

"Is anything too difficult for the LORD? At the appointed time I will return to you, at this time next year, and Sarah will have a son." (Genesis 18:14)

"I know that You can do all things,
And that no purpose of Yours can be thwarted." (Job 42:2)

"Ah Lord GOD! Behold, You have made the heavens and the earth by Your great power and by Your outstretched arm! Nothing is too difficult for You," (Jeremiah 32:17)

"Looking at them, Jesus said, 'With people it is impossible, but not with God; for all things are possible with God.'" (Mark 10:27)

"For nothing will be impossible with God." (Luke 1:37)

"But He said, 'The things that are impossible with people are possible with God.'" (Luke 18:27)

"OK," I say. So, bottom-line, all things are possible with God. If I am to walk, again, it is up to Him… and of course Him working through the physical therapists and doctors to help me. And, He called upon others around me to share words of encouragement to help me retain a positive frame of mind. I am an optimistic person, but there were days…

Putting the pieces into place…

Consider this idea. Scripture tells us that God is the potter and we are the clay.

"But now, O Lord, You are our Father,
We are the clay, and You our potter;
And all of us are the work of Your hand."(Isaiah 64:8)

Obviously, my body… my "earthen vessel" had been shattered and was in need of further repair. The surgeons rebuilt me with metal parts. Now, it was time for me to learn how to use those parts while simultaneously rebuilding the muscle masses that had atrophied since the wreck, due to my immobilized state. Being air-ambulanced to that rehabilitation facility in Richmond, Virginia, to begin a program of intensive physical therapy reminds me of this scripture:

"Draw for yourself water for the siege!
Strengthen your fortifications!
Go into the clay and tread the mortar!
Take hold of the brick mold!" (Nahum 3:14)

Each day, I would work with the physical therapist to try to regain use of my legs and arm. Those days were long and painful. There were days where I progressed toward recovery and days where I regressed. I needed to realize what we are told in 1Peter 5:7 "casting all your anxiety on Him, because He cares for you." My cousin, Maria, moved from Marietta, Georgia, up to Virginia, just to help us during my rehabilitation. She was talking with me one day when I was feeling down about having a bad day at physical therapy, and I was very upset about my legs and arm not working. The physical therapist was trying to teach me how to get my limbs to respond to what my brain was telling them to do… like re-training the spinal nervous system… interesting experience. My cousin pointed out to me that I was "the only impatient procrastinator she knew." Think about that – I can be puzzling to people. I just wanted to get out of the wheelchair and care for my babies… and care for myself… I could not physically do anything for anyone. I just wanted to be renewed… physically and spiritually.

"For to me, to live is Christ, and to die is gain." (Philippians 1:21)

My vanity, perfectionism, and blissful façade, had all been shattered… along with my car. In Beth Moore's book *Discovering God's Purpose for Your Life*,[1] she talks of times when everything is being stripped away in our lives so that we must focus on God. He is all we have. I felt as if I had died on the outside. All that was left were some shattered limbs, a beating heart, a mind with a lot of questions, and some organs inside. We had wanted to have another baby. I was on prenatal vitamins when the car wreck happened. Through all of this brokenness, would I ever be able to conceive and carry a child… would I even be able to physically care for my baby twins?

Between physical therapy sessions, through my tears I would try to pray. Jesus tells us how:

"Pray, then, in this way:

'Our Father who is in heaven,
Hallowed be Your name.
Your kingdom come.
Your will be done,
On earth as it is in heaven.
Give us this day our daily bread.
And forgive us our debts, as we also have forgiven our debtors.
And do not lead us into temptation, but deliver us from evil. [For Yours is the kingdom and the power and the glory forever. Amen.]'

And know that... For if you forgive others for their transgressions, your heavenly Father will also forgive you. But if you do not forgive others, then your Father will not forgive your transgressions." (Matthew 6:7-15)

I pray that your earthen vessel be filled with God's treasures and that your face is radiant with His love. Forgiving others and asking forgiveness from people whom we have wronged are two important links in building our chain of relationships.

Unveiling the view…

I needed to remove the figurative "bejeweled veil" and look both inside and around me to see God's almighty presence in my life. He was, is, and always will be with us 24/7. He is alive and ready for us to seek Him. We are all called to be servant-leaders just as Phil Hodges and Ken Blanchard illustrate in their book *Lead Like Jesus*.[2]

Pray about the following message found in Matthew 6:24–34:

"No one can serve two masters; for either he will hate the one and love the other, or he will be devoted to one and despise the other. You cannot serve God and wealth. For this reason I say to you, do not be worried about your life, *as to* what you will eat or what you will drink; nor for your body, *as to* what you will put on. Is not life more than food, and the body more than clothing? Look at the birds of the air, that they do not sow, nor reap nor gather into barns, and *yet* your heavenly Father feeds them. Are you not worth much more than they? And who of you by being worried can add a *single* hour to his life? And why are you worried about clothing? Observe how the lilies of the field grow; they do not toil nor do they spin, yet I say to you that not even Solomon in all his glory clothed himself like one of these. But if God so clothes the grass of the field, which is *alive* today and tomorrow is thrown into the furnace, *will He* not much more *clothe* you? You of little faith! Do not worry then, saying, 'What will we eat?' or 'What will we drink?' or 'What will we wear for clothing?' For the Gentiles eagerly seek all these things; for your heavenly Father knows that you need all these things. But seek first His kingdom and His righteousness, and all these things will be added to you. So do not worry about tomorrow; for tomorrow will care for itself. Each day has enough trouble of its own."

God is calling us to serve and lead… to evangelize…calmly and courageously.

Is there a piece missing? Filling in the cracks…

Remember these words…

"Cast your burden upon the Lord and He will sustain you; He will never allow the righteous to be shaken." (Psalm 55:22)

"Each one helps his neighbor
And says to his brother, 'Be strong!'
So the craftsman encourages the smelter,
And he who smooths *metal* with the hammer *encourages* him who beats the anvil,
Saying of the soldering, 'It is good';
And he fastens it with nails,
So that it will not totter." (Isaiah 41:6-7)

Know that the Lord will carry us when we need Him to do so. But, also recognize the need for us to help each other – both in word and in action.

Smoothing the rough edges…

Our lives ebb and flow in waves of renewal and redemption as long as we keep our eyes on Jesus. If we yearn to be filled with and taste the essence of the Holy Spirit, we experience what Paul shares with us in 2 Corinthians 3:17-18… "Now the Lord is the Spirit, and where the Spirit of the Lord is, *there* is liberty. But we all, with unveiled face, beholding as in a mirror the glory of the Lord, are being transformed into the same image from glory to glory, just as from the Lord, the Spirit." Each morning, as I prayerfully seek direction for the day, I go down on my knees to thank our Lord for His many blessings and ask that He will carry me though this day. I still live with pain in my knees, legs, and arm, but with God's grace, I have learned that "it is all relative," i.e., relative to the distress my body and soul were in at the time of the wreck. The pain now is so minimal compared to the pain then. God has taught me to re-focus my energy toward Him and His will for my life. And, that prognosis is so much more exciting than dwelling on the aches and potential functional limitations. I think God blessed me with the gift of perseverance (determination? stubbornness at times?) and expected reaction to a faceable challenge to see what choices I will make when confronted with a test. Will I retreat or will I pray in search of His direction for the task? Since the wreck, I admit that I view obstacles quite a bit differently. To put it bluntly, stuff happens for a reason… "Life is not about waiting for the storm to pass. It's about learning to dance in the rain." [Vivian Greene] When challenges come along, no matter the size, I prayerfully ask God what to do next. How should I respond to the circumstances placed before me? He will walk us through the embers and carry us when necessary. We just need to ask Him. "But as for me, I trust in You, O Lord, I say, "You are my God." (Psalm 31:14)

When we feel stuck…patience… fear… and fire...

There were times during my recovery when either my knee or arm joints would not function at all or they would become locked or "stuck" in a certain position. I remember when my arm was stuck in a bent 30 degree position and my hand would not move at all. The physical therapist was working with me and my goal was to pick up a Cheerio… which I could not do for quite some time. During that time, both of my legs were not functioning at all, and then my right knee locked in a slightly bent position. The physical therapist taught us how to strap my left arm and both legs into CPM machines that would move the joints for me since I had no control over their movement. When my knee became stuck, that CPM machine trying to bend and straighten it for me was excruciating.

Then, the physical therapist recruited my cousin (who was living with us to help take care of the babies) and my father-in-law (who was visiting) to help straighten my right leg. Here was the assignment: Five times every day, we would roll my wheelchair over to a straight chair, pick up my right leg and place my heel on the chair so that there was nothing but air below my knee. Then, the person whose turn it was to help me, would put one hand palm down directly above my knee and the other hand palm down directly below my knee, and then push as hard as he/she could and hold it for ten seconds. Then release and do it again, for five reps. They would do that whole procedure five different times every day… 25 experiences every day. You can imagine the physical pain involved with each set of pushes… and my relatives' emotional pain when they saw me hurting while they were working to follow the physical therapist's instructions. My father-in-law apologized to me every time it was his turn, and my cousin prayed over my knee before each pushing session.

Philippians 3:13 - 14 instructs us: Brethren, I do not regard myself as having laid hold of *it* yet; but one thing *I do*: forgetting what *lies* behind and reaching forward to what *lies* ahead, I press on toward the goal for the prize of the upward call of God in Christ Jesus.

Then, it came time for another surgery on my rebuilt foot, and while under anesthesia, my orthopaedic surgeon unlocked my knee. Within a few days, it locked up, again. So, when it was time for surgery on my rebuilt foot, again, my orthopaedic surgeon unlocked my knee, again, and while still in a wheelchair, I tried my best to move it using my right hand to lift and push down to straighten the limb, as continuously as I could to keep the joint from freezing up as it did after the previous surgery. I was still going to physical therapy every day.

Miracles…
Miracles happened during my recovery – things such as a bacterial infection infecting every patient in the trauma ICU, except for me. My internal injuries from the wreck included my liver being cut and bleeding. The trauma surgeon opened me up and it suddenly stopped bleeding. So, she just closed me back up. There was a time after I had already been air ambulanced to Virginia, when we realized that the doctor in Tennessee had accidentally left a staple in my abdomen – visible from the outside. Multiple nurses and my new primary care physician confirmed this observation to be true. So, he rolled me into an exam room that could accommodate a wheelchair patient – the exam table would be lowered so I could transfer onto it with help. Then, he doused the area on my abdomen that contained the staple with a topical anesthetic and told me that he would come back in about 20 minutes to remove the staple. As I was lying there, I began to sob. I told my husband, who was there holding my hand, that I could not go through another medical procedure at that point… my emotional state was not good. My husband asked me to pray with him. We prayed that God would carry me through this experience and help me to rely on His strength. When the doctor returned, he said he needed to wipe away the excess anesthetic so that he could then remove the surgical staple. He wiped off the liquid and the staple was gone. The doctor and nurses were speechless. As my husband rolled my wheelchair out of the office and to the car that day, we were praising God for this miracle.

Through God's grace and prayerful perseverance, I did learn to walk, again… physically and spiritually. And, I regained use of my left arm and hand. Oh, the joy I felt to be able to pick up my babies once again! As far as writing, I have heard that "God does not call the qualified. He qualifies the called." [Author unknown] So, for two years, three months, and seventeen days, I worked with God's direction to write *Navigate with God*[3] and the accompanying workbook. God is currently leading me through the composition of a Christian fiction novel series focused on the spiritual gifts. First book in the series is *Blue-Eyed Ruse.*[4] With experiences in the roles of inspirational speaker, professor, author, television show host, and producer, I feel blessed to have opportunities to share true stories about God's love, mercy, grace, and healing. There are numerous adaptations to the idea that "It's not what happens to you, but rather what you do with what happens to you." I continue to seek God's direction for new ways to share His message.

Proverbs 16:1-4: "The plans of the heart belong to man,
But the answer of the tongue is from the Lord.
All the ways of a man are clean in his own sight,
But the Lord weighs the motives.
Commit your works to the Lord
And your plans will be established.
The Lord has made everything for its own purpose,"

All things are possible with God…
With faith at least the size of a mustard seed (upon reading this scripture, out of curiosity I researched mustard seeds… they are small!), we can move mountains and carry out God's will (paraphrased from Matthew 17:20). Wow! So, what if our faith is bigger than a mustard seed… then, we can come to recognize that "all things are possible with God" (in Matthew 19:26). I know this truth because God saved my life and my babies' lives. We are walking miracles of His grace, faith, mercy, and healing. There were so many people praying for us. The power of prayer is unsurpassed in accomplishment. I believe that nothing is impossible to those who believe.

"And Jesus said to him, 'If You can? All things are possible to him who believes.' Immediately the boy's father cried out and said, 'I do believe; help my unbelief.'" (Mark 9:23-24) And, I did learn to walk again. I learned to walk the same month that my toddler twins did – in the race to walk, I came in third!

To paraphrase Romans 12:2, we are being called not to conform to this world, but rather to be transformed according to God's purpose. God opened my eyes to His presence during the recovery transformation. So, now at this point with gradual improvement in the use of my legs, the questions: how much physical integrity has this earthen vessel lost? And, what is the expected restoration percentage? How well will this earthen vessel function and is it (am I) willing to open up and be filled with God's treasures? Let's continue the journey.

Beginning again… now with a proclamation…
F. Scott Fitzgerald, famous American author, said "Vitality shows not only in the ability to persist, but in the ability to start over again."

As I surf along the crests and troughs of the waves of change and renewal in my life, I sometimes reflect on the challenges I have experienced thus far. In particular, the timeline of life experiences since June 15, 2000, differs dramatically from the predictions of the doctors on that very day. Actually, I do physically surf and water ski… and the doctors said I would never walk again. God had other plans for my life. He has called me to embrace His love and proclaim a freedom from fear in the name of Christ. I proclaim to live each day without fear, and with my eyes, ears, heart, soul, and mind open to the leadings of the Holy Spirit. As I learn to live in freedom from fear, I give my life over to God with amplified and complete trust in His promises, and I am to be filled with relentless thanksgiving for His love and approach to peace in my life. In 2 Timothy 1:7 we are called to be fearless, i.e., "For God has not given us a spirit of timidity, but of power and love and discipline."

Christ is ever present in our lives and He is there as an example for us to follow. He is there to lead us in becoming servant/leaders for God... to build His Kingdom here on earth... in readying ourselves and those around us for welcome into His eternal heavenly kingdom. He is calling us to walk with Him.

Michael W. Smith shares this message in the song "I'm Waiting for You"[5] where Jesus is telling us that we are not alone.

Our earthen vessels are filled with God's treasure. My vessel is not perfect, but God's treasures are perfect...His love, grace, mercy, and kindness. I pray every day that He will show me the way in which He wants me to share the treasures that He has entrusted to me. "O God, You are my God; I shall seek You earnestly; My soul thirsts for You," (Psalm 63:1)

Miracle of life...

More miracles... it was two years after my total hip replacement. Hurricane Isabelle was blowing through Richmond, Virginia. A friend of ours, Brenda Gemmell, who is the Joint Replacement Coordinator at the hospital where I had my hip surgery, and she knew we were planning to deliver our new baby girl at that same hospital, was walking into the hospital at the time of the hurricane. There was no power – just an emergency generator at the hospital for emergency surgeries – and no fresh water. As she was walking into a dark hospital on that autumn morning, she noticed that there was a larger than usual number of people hurrying into the hospital. Then, she realized that these were expectant couples and she remembered that changes in barometric pressure can bring on labor. Next, she thought about me and my husband being pregnant, and she said that she suddenly exclaimed out loud to anyone within ear shot, "If anyone would have a baby during a hurricane, it would be Ginny Frings!" Well, guess what – I did! Kristen Maria Frings was born at 10:33 p.m. on that same day.

God calls us to be disciples for Him and to help grow His kingdom. After surviving three near death experiences in my life, including the doctors telling my parents that since I was premature and Mother was hemorrhaging so badly, that I would be stillborn – he would do all he could to save my mother, but he would not be able to save me; going into remission from a terminal illness when I was only 7 years old; and, then the car crash of 2000. I am still here for a reason. God has plans.

I am reminded of Hebrews 12:12-13: "Therefore, strengthen the hands that are weak and the knees that are feeble, and make straight paths for your feet, so that *the limb* which is lame may not be put out of joint, but rather be healed." I am praying. Messages that come to mind are those contained within Steven Curtis Chapman's song "Way Beyond the Blue,"[6] and Michael W. Smith's song "Rise."[7] I am trying to answer our Father's call.

Galatians 6:9: "Let us not lose heart in doing good, for in due time we will reap if we do not grow weary."

∆∆∆∆∆ *Focus on the Lift* ∆∆∆∆∆

We read about the use of earthen vessels in the Bible. What if we apply the idea that we are all earthen vessels - at times shattered and broken - to our own lives. What do you feel God calling you to do in your life? In due time… in His time… yes… God's calling out to you.

"You said, 'Behold, the LORD our God has shown us His glory and His greatness, and we have heard His voice from the midst of the fire; we have seen today that God speaks with man, yet he lives.'" (Deuteronomy 5:24)

***

Chapter 6
∞∞∞∞∞∞ Invitation ∞∞∞∞∞∞

"Just remaining quietly in the presence of God, listening to Him, being attentive to Him, requires a lot of courage and know-how."---Thomas Merton

INVITATION
by Albert Cloudy

A Gift given to you by God
The unimaginable… the unexpected
With a mind hard to comprehend the chance
Your heart drops in excitement
The Prayer you gave to the Man upstairs
Which was answered in time of need
When all hopes were lost
He may not be there when you want Him
But He is always on time
To give you grace
To achieve fulfillment
In the life path that was planned for you
With an opportunity more Grand than anything
That took that burden off your shoulders
And relieved that stress of what to do next
With Faith and believing in Him

There will be many more miracles
Opportunities that you don't think you deserve
That's all because God leaves no one behind!

©2016 Albert Cloudy. All rights reserved. Used with permission.

He is the Potter… we are the clay…
Now, let's visit an art studio… God's studio where He is the Master Potter and we are the clay.

When one works with clay to form pottery, there are certain materials needed. Physically sculpting with clay to make a piece of pottery requires:

- Clay
- Water
- Preparation
- Fire
- Time

This analogy provokes one to consider a life application to the art of creating clay sculptures and pottery. Consider this thought: Just like when working with clay, we require life-giving water to sustain us. Everything we do in life requires some type of preparation. There are times when we feel as if we are being burned and refined by fire (difficult situations). And, we often complain about not having enough time – or when we are waiting for something to happen, needing greater patience. So, we are in fact earthen vessels of clay just as Paul speaks of in 2Corinthians. When we walk with Paul and recognize that we are in fact earthen vessels being readied to carry God's treasures, it can be a very humbling realization on two fronts: first of all, the fact that we are globs of clay awaiting the hand of God to mold and shape us into His image; and secondly, that He would entrust us with so precious a gift as His treasure. The treasure that God wants to make come alive within us is His Spirit. Through the death and resurrection of His Son, Jesus

Christ, we are invited to "Come to the Table" and share in the blood and body of the Almighty. We are called to follow the path of salvation with the eternal reward in Heaven. I just keep straying from the path, and then find myself seeking renewal as God shares His grace with me, just like MercyMe sings about in "The First Time." [1]

Life is fragile...

Have you seen the bumper sticker that reads: "Life is fragile. Handle with prayer."? For the most part, we are fragile beings. Sociologists study humankind from many different perspectives, including physical, emotional, relational, familial, and spiritual. Now, keep that in mind as we return to Paul's message to us. Pottery, i.e., earthen vessels are fragile. They can be broken. We can be broken. So, we as earthen vessels are basically fragile in nature. We need to rely on the Lord's strength to continue in this world. When we break, most of us tend to feel distraught, angry, and embarrassed... the whole "how could this happen to me – I am stronger than this" routine. I have learned that in our brokenness, we can learn of God's strength, 2Corinthians 13:9 tells us " For we rejoice when we ourselves are weak but you are strong; this we also pray for, that you be made complete."

So, in our weakness, God enters with His strength to help us handle our circumstances. His resilience reigns and rains over us like a cloak. God's shield and armor (Ephesians 6) are tools we can prayerfully don each day and invite God to fill us with His grace, cover our weaknesses, and carry us through the obstacles of the day. When I was broken, physically and spiritually, Jesus taught me through the people around me that He is here beckoning us to invite Him into ourselves and become filled with His Spirit. What an awesome feeling to know that God wants to be the thread that joins us all together as His family! When we accept His invitation, we begin to become aware of His constant presence and His grace.

Ginny W. Frings, Ph.D.

Gathering... planting... gathering...
Where can we find "seeds of compassion"? As Jesus teaches us in the Bible, He and His Father embrace us with compassion, but often we are unaware of their presence. In our own "laser-focused" worlds of existence, we may not recognize those seeds of compassion sprinkled around us. Those seeds can come in the form of what I like to call "Golden Moments" of discernment when - we cross paths with the right person at the right time, times when difference-making ideas suddenly come to mind, Scriptures and messages enter our lives at the precise time needed to help us or someone else, or times when the solution comes to us before the problem arises. These experiences are God's leadings and presence before us, just waiting to be planted, tended, and harvested. During tending and harvesting, vegetation tends to produce and release seeds for the next generation of growth. As we gather and plant God's seeds of compassion and forgiveness in our lives, what will the fruit yield look like? What about abundance? Spiritual and physical "climate" can affect the output. Ask God to guide your horticultural efforts.

Scatter or poke?...
I remember learning how to plant one of my favorite flowers, nasturtiums, when I was 5 years old. One sunny day, my Daddy and I went to the nearby garden store where we lived in Texas, and we learned how to prepare the soil, plant each individual nasturtium seed by poking a single hole (about the depth of my little index finger) and dropping one seed into the hole. Next, we covered and patted the dirt over each seed, and delicately watered the row of seeds. We then vigilantly tended the garden by weeding and watering as needed during the germination and gestation period. Then, one day... I ran to the garden when I got home from kindergarten and there were little leaves popping up through the soil. I was so excited. I ran to tell Mother and I could not wait for Daddy to come home from work that evening to see the new leaves! Then, we continued to care for the plants and blooms appeared... eventually opening to reveal beautiful yellow, red, and orange flowers on a backdrop of bright green leaves. Mother brought her easel and oil paints outside to the garden so she could paint some vibrant flowerscapes. All of her

nasturtium garden paintings have sold in art shows through the years… paintings of God's colorful artwork… inspiring. While living in La Jolla, Mother and I would plant another flower called alyssum with its varying hues of purple mixed with white, and quite fragrant. Alyssum seeds are so small that the "scatter technique" is more appropriate for planting that type of seed.

Lord, Master Gardener, we seek You in this planting season…
Are you aware of the heavenly seeds of compassion which God has placed before you? People or situations where you could share compassion… or where you could reap compassion when you are in need? If yes, let's begin gathering and planting. If no, let's pray about sharpening our awareness of Scriptural clues and the people around us - either who are trying to help others or who are in need of compassion themselves. The opportunities to sow the seeds of compassion are there…just look and dialogue with God for direction. He will lead you to your garden spot… it could be next door, or right in your own front yard.

High Tea… accepting God's invitation…
While praying about the direction for this book, a message of "compassion" kept coming to mind. Then, while enjoying some tea one morning while writing, I felt the invitation from God to share a "cup of compassion" with Him and Jesus. But, He said, it was up to me to sow the seeds, harvest the leaves, and prepare them for drying, in anticipation of the family gathering. Wow! I had so many questions. Then, it felt as though the Holy Spirit began to work within me to decipher the message. What are seeds of compassion – times when we have the opportunity to listen and be supportive of others – times we can relate and encourage others because we have experienced similar situations. And, there can be seeds of compassion planted within us by God that help us to know His presence. Then, we can be called to share those seeds with other people. What seeds of compassion were evident in my life and what seeds were missing? What seeds had I kept to myself and what seeds had I shared with others? Those are tough questions to answer and when we do get to the answers, the responses

can cause us to realize that we have more seeds of compassion to sow before the harvest. Earlier, we talked about planting seeds of compassion and praying about how to become more aware of others who need compassion in their lives. Here, we are building upon this idea. Let's prepare for High Tea with the Almighty… first step… plant the seeds in preparation for harvest.

∆∆∆∆∆ *Focus on the Lift* ∆∆∆∆∆

Planting seeds of compassion…
What do your seeds of compassion look like? What do and will your plants look like while growing in your garden of compassion? Will they bear flowers and fruit? Will the leaves be abundant and full of compassion for others or will they be lacking and sparse? How will your garden be nourished and grow? Draw a picture of your garden of compassion. Are there people in your life waiting for your seeds of compassion to germinate and grow? Describe the seeds of compassion you will be sowing in preparation for the harvest. What are seeds of compassion? Ponder this: Are there people in your life – friends or acquaintances who need some compassion right now? Are they struggling with earthly responsibilities? How do you define compassion? Merriam Webster defines compassion as: "sympathetic consciousness of others' distress together with a desire to alleviate it."[2] So, practicing active listening skills, as taught in Chapter 4 of *Navigate with God*,[3] helps us to plant the seeds of compassion… of awareness and action toward a plan of distress mitigation. Ask Jesus to help you increase your awareness of others' obstacles… perceived or real… and to then guide you in ways to help them work toward a solution.

***

You've got mail…
God, Jesus, and the Holy Spirit have extended an invitation to all of us on earth, and They eagerly await each of our acceptances to

Their invitation to everlasting life… an invitation to High Tea with the Almighty. How will you reply? How will your R.S.V.P. read? And, when will it arrive?

God is inviting us to be with Him and His Son… to sow the seeds of compassion and grow them. After tending and harvesting, the leaves can be dried and steeped to fill our cups of compassion to be shared with others. We are invited to sit at the table with God and Jesus. In the song entitled, "Come to the Table"[4] by Michael Card, Jesus is inviting us all to sit with Him at the table. Remember, at the Last Supper table, there were two disciples in particular – one who would deny knowing Jesus multiple times, and one who would betray Him and completely go astray. Jesus knew of the future, and still He invited, loved, and died for all of them there that evening… and for all of us. Accept The invitation. Come be with The Trinity and enjoy some tea… no real need to R.S.V.P.… They already know your plans.

God is the potter… we are the clay…
Relaxing with a cup of tea can be an occasional treat in life's busy schedule. In this chapter, we will learn how to relax with Jesus when we accept His invitation to High Tea… where we will share a cup of compassion with the Lord. But, before we fill our cup, we need to first ask God to help us fashion our cup. We are the clay and God is the potter, molding us in His image and shaping us for His purpose. Think about that… are you willing to let God be your designer? Remember, He created the world. Let Him shape and polish you. Ralph Waldo Emerson said, "The purpose of life is not to be happy. It is to be useful, to be honorable, to be compassionate, to have it make some difference that you have lived and lived well."

Yesterday, in church, we were singing the song by Michael W. Smith entitled "Mighty To Save"[5] about God's compassion, strength, and gift of His Son for our salvation… powerful song. In this chapter, we will be asking God to help us fill ourselves and our cups with His compassion.

Ginny W. Frings, Ph.D.

Before we can put our clay on the potter's wheel, we first need to journey over to the rushing stream and dig up the clay. Then, we will work and knead the clay… vetting out any rocks and shale to soften it. Let's start hiking…

ΔΔΔΔ *Focus on the Lift* ΔΔΔΔ

The art of compassion…
Open your mind and close your eyes: It has just rained and the stream is alive. As we seek our source of clay on the grassy banks, a school of golden trout swim by… beautiful. Can you feel the coolness and mist in the air after the storm? It feels nice. Then, you spy some natural clay – grey and tan in varying hues – near a tree trunk at the water's edge. You begin digging and find that it is not easy. You seek and find a larger stick with a beveled end to better extract the wet clay from its habitat. When you have gathered enough clay, thinking about the size of cup you would like to craft, and taking into consideration that mixed in with the clay is expected to be some pebbles and shale rock, you relax beside the rushing water for a few moments. On a piece of paper, sketch a picture of your clay cup. This sketch will become a rendering of Your Cup of Compassion. This cup contains the kinds of compassion you will share with others. What does your cup of compassion look like? Is it tall? Short? Colorful? Plain? Bejeweled? Is it filled with words? Quotes? Scriptures? Pictures? Experiences? Stories? Goals? Regrets or Do-overs? Now, let's thank God for this opportunity and ask Him to guide us on our journey of compassion. When you are ready, let's get back onto the trail of *Titanium Transformation*. There are mountains to climb and rivers to ford.

***

On a mountain top…
As we prepare to respond to the invitation for High Tea with the Almighty, let's take some time to consider not only the significance of Jesus' teaching in mountain venues, but also the magnitude - grand

in significance - of God's gift of water for quenching our thirst… physiologically and spiritually.

In the Bible, we read many stories recounting experiences and interactions with God while disciples and prophets were climbing up or traveling through mountainous terrain.

Sometimes life can feel like an uphill journey… as if we are trying to climb to the summit. While backpacking through the mountains, both in the United States and Europe, my husband and I would come across stacks of rocks… appearing to be carefully placed on top of the others, as if signifying something. According to legend, you are supposed to stop and place a stone on each pillar of rocks as you pass to let others know that hikers have traveled this path, and to encourage them to stay on the path and keep climbing. Contemplate this idea: how can we encourage each other to persevere on the path of life?

I am a better "downhill hiker," meaning that I do not climb mountains very quickly… to uh…let's say, give myself time to enjoy the scenery? Do you buy that excuse? Anyway, my husband's quote when we are hiking uphill on a mountain trail while I, the shutterbug, am snapping photos all the way up the trail, is: "Ginny, just keep hiking. The view at the top of the trail will be even more beautiful." Let's keep climbing in search of that view… the scenic overlook God has prepared for us.

The water and photosynthesis…
Now, we will get back to our task of planting and harvesting. To grow seeds of compassion, we need water. Recall the story of Jesus at the water well with the Samaritan woman. Jesus is calling us to change our thinking and perceptions about people and the roles others play in our lives… bringing about awareness… compassion… opening a door… helping us to follow a particular path… calling us to be mirrors of God's love. Invite His message into your heart.

Miracles and witnessing of compassion…

Ginny W. Frings, Ph.D.

Healing a Nobleman's Son

Therefore He came again to Cana of Galilee where He had made the water wine And there was a royal official whose son was sick at Capernaum.

When he heard that Jesus had come out of Judea into Galilee, he went to Him and was imploring Him to come down and heal his son; for he was at the point of death.

So Jesus said to him, "Unless you people see signs and wonders, you simply will not believe."

The royal official said to Him, "Sir, come down before my child dies."

Jesus said to him, "Go; your son lives." The man believed the word that Jesus spoke to him and started off.

As he was now going down, his slaves met him, saying that his son was living.

So he inquired of them the hour when he began to get better. Then they said to him, "Yesterday at the seventh hour the fever left him."

So the father knew that it was at that hour in which Jesus said to him, "Your son lives"; and he himself believed and his whole household.

This is again a second sign that Jesus performed when He had come out of Judea into Galilee. [John 4:46-54]

Jesus performed many miracles as testimony to His Father's love, grace, and compassion. As we journey on the path in search of life-giving water, God calls us to plant the seeds of faith and compassion along the way. The father in the verses above had faith so great that he believed Jesus could heal his dying son. And, his son was healed.

Contemplate your faith. Is it rooted? Are you tending it? Is it growing? Will you be ready for the harvest?

A new perspective of compassion…
In times of difficulty, we often tend to place blame on someone or something who we believe to be (justified or not) the reason for our strife. Recall something that Jesus said while being crucified: "Father, forgive them; for they do not know what they are doing." And they cast lots, dividing up His garments among themselves. [Luke 23:34] Jesus is a beautiful example of walking in the fruit of compassion. Think about this… is there need of compassion in your life? As givers of compassion, we can become recipients of redemption.

Changes in behavior and expectations…
When a loved one begins to be hurtful toward family members - whether emotionally or physically - it is a difficult condition to endure. Recently, a friend began telling me her story of emotional torment by her spouse. She and her husband were experiencing difficult economic times. His thoughtless comments and raised tones were hurting the whole family. My friend's daughter was asking her why Daddy fights with her so much. She did not have an answer. The day she called, she and her child had been yelled at and chastised from morning until night on that particular Saturday. That next morning, my friend's husband had attempted to apologize to her, but then continued the verbal rampage aimed at her and their daughter. My friend had been in tears most of the day and did not know where to turn for help. She said she was trying to pray, but did not know what to ask for. She finally decided to call me and said, "At least if he was hitting me, I could call the police for help… yes, it would hurt, but cuts and bruises can heal… emotional scars are difficult to handle for other reasons," she said. "With his hurtful words and behavior, I just have to put up with it for the rest of my life… for my child's sake."

At first, I did not know what to say to my friend. Then, these words came to mind: "God can heal people and relationships. Ask Him to change your husband's heart. God is near. Invite Him to intervene and give you guidance for your situation. Talk with your family. Work together to mitigate the relationship disfunctionality and give your lives to Christ. He knows the way to everlasting joy." Then, we prayed. She seemed to have some renewed hope. Mending the family relationships will take time. Remember, Galatians 6:9 teaches us:

"Let us not lose heart in doing good, for in due time we will reap if we do not grow weary."

ΔΔΔΔΔ   *Focus on the Lift*   ΔΔΔΔΔ

We all experience situations each day where we are given the opportunity to be compassionate and understanding with someone – a family member, friend, coworker, acquaintance, or pet. Or, we learn of someone's needs through the news or in an article. For the next seven days, write down the name(s) or groups of individuals you hear about needing some compassion. Then, write down a plan of action for helping them. The requests could range from the need for someone to listen, some encouragement, biological needs such as food, shelter, clothing, a friend, a "break in the day" just to talk, or making a phone call to someone with the knowledge or skills to help the person (e.g., you know the perfect repair person to fix your aunt's sink). Whatever difficulty the person is experiencing, even if you are not "the" answer, you can be an instrument or facilitator on the path to the solution. Just take the time to look at the situation with new eyes and have compassion.

***

Live out loud…
God has asked us to be His disciples. As we learn to be more aware of God's presence in our lives, we can learn how to be witnesses to His grace each day. Through the birth, death, and resurrection of His Son, He has exhibited His unconditional love and presence for us. Think

about the prophets of the B.C. era. Their faith in God was so immense and they communicated directly with Him… and they foretold the coming of the Messiah because they believed the message God was sending to them. And, then contemplate the faith and obedience of God's followers such as Noah, Moses, Abraham, and his son, Isaac. And, what about Mary… the unfaltering love and belief in the goodness of God enabled her to help bring forth Jesus, the Messiah, about whom the prophets had been speaking. Pray this scripture with me and ask God to help us be His disciples and "live out loud" in His presence.

"who has saved us and called us with a holy calling, not according to our works, but according to His own purpose and grace which was granted us in Christ Jesus from all eternity," [2Timothy 1:9]

The tallest angel…
While I was growing up in La Jolla, California, my mother was an avid seascape artist and earned much recognition for her artwork. One summer day, Mother was painting, while my friend Kristie and I (age 9) were playing at the beach known as Children's Beach (thus named because there was a rock jetty that blocked the waves from reaching the shore; therefore, keeping the swimming area waters calm and safe for young swimmers. Today, that very beach is known as "Seal beach" because it has become a seal habitat – I have never seen so many seals in one location napping in the sun and playing in the calm waters). We enjoyed a nice day and later that afternoon, Kristie and I became a bit adventurous. Kristie took the lead on climbing a particular boulder near the shore. As she reached the top, I began the ascent and then decided that with the later tide rising, our best plan of action would be for Kristie to climb down instead of me climbing up. But, and justifiably so, she became frightened with the rising water. Suddenly, a stranger, the tallest person I have ever met, walked over to us and asked if he could help. Kristie was barely able to climb down onto the gentleman's shoulders and he carried her to safety away from the water's edge. Mother came running over and thanked the stranger for helping us. We asked if he lived nearby and he told us he was a tourist.

Today, Kristie has her own beautiful family and she works as a dermatologist in La Jolla. Instead of selling the painting of Children's Beach that Mother created that day, she gave it to me and it has hung in my room over the years. Now, the painting, entitled "Kristie's rock," hangs in my dining room here in St. Louis and will grace the cover of one of my future books. Friends and visitors to our home often inquire about the beautiful piece of artwork, giving us the opportunity to share the story of "the tallest angel." God is always near.

∆∆∆∆∆ *Focus on the Lift* ∆∆∆∆∆

Angels are in our lives. Close your eyes and recall some times in your life where someone came along unexpectedly and helped you work through a situation where you needed some help, but you did not know where to turn for assistance. Thoughtfully, write down these experiences. Then, pray for awareness of and gratitude for the angels whom God sends to us.

***

Who are you... ?
Nearly three years after the car wreck, we were blessed to give birth to a baby girl. Five months after her birth, we began consulting with Bill Jiranek, M.D., the orthopedic surgeon who had performed a very successful total hip replacement for me in 2001, about potential corrections for continual problems with my ankle and knees. My knee and ankle problems had been intensifying since the car wreck – or either were more noticeable since my other injuries had since healed. On the conservative side, Bill generally likes to prescribe physical therapy for patients either as a solution to the ailment, or in preparation for a needed surgical procedure. So, Bill prescribed a physical therapy (PT) regimen for me and recommended I consult with a physical therapist named Rick Herod in Richmond. I agreed to undergo PT, but I was determined to return to the PT who had taught me how to walk again and regain use

of my arm and hand after the car wreck, nearly three years earlier. When I called her office, I learned that she was on maternity leave. So, I went with Bill's recommendation and scheduled an appointment with Rick. While there on the first visit (with our youngest daughter who was only five months old at the time and in the stroller), I was exercising one of my knees at the PT's instruction, and I was talking with other patients. Then, this very nice lady came over to me, smiling, and said, "You are here exercising your leg, playing with your baby, smiling, and talking. Who are you?" I graciously told her. Then, she proceeded to introduce herself and I began to put the pieces together. She was Susan Reynolds of the Reynolds Aluminum family who lived right there in Richmond, Virginia. Interestingly, we both had the same orthopedic surgeon, Dr. Bill Jiranek. Then, before she left the PT office, she walked over to me and my baby and said, "Ginny, I believe people meet for a reason. I think I'm supposed to help you with your car seat safety program. Let me have your card." I gave her my card. We soon met and developed a working relationship and friendship during the years we lived in Richmond. The Randolph and Susan Reynolds Foundation enabled us to help many parents learn how to properly install their children's car seats and travel more safely in the car. Susan and her family helped provide new car seats to families who needed them and helped save many lives. God and His angels are all around us.

∆∆∆∆∆   *Focus on the Lift*   ∆∆∆∆∆

In the song "A New Hallelujah,"[6] Michael W. Smith sings about our need to arise and become witnesses for God to let every nation know of His nearness. God is near. We need to receive Him and proclaim His closeness. My mother's written prayer and Toby Mac's song, "Speak Life,"[7] encourage all of us to lift each other up, rather than tear others down. Speak life. Know that words can hurt and words can heal.

For seven days, make a list of your daily experiences and people you meet. Ask God to help us see His presence in these experiences and acquaintances. How do you feel? Write down those reflections and insights.

***

Next, we will investigate the role of intuition while deepening our relationship with God, and learn how to strengthen and broaden our relationships with the people surrounding us. Jesus invites us to walk with Him every day as we try to traverse the gaps in our relationships… swim the turbulent waters… climb the sometimes disparaging paths laden with what feels like boulders of hindrances on our travels toward the peak - if we can even see it through the cloud cover. Let's prayerfully embrace the idea that God's grace awaits you. He is inviting you to join Him on the journey. Welcome His presence.

INTUITION
by Albert Cloudy

You whisper in my ear as you tell your secret
But before this day you didn't know I noticed
The way you changed and the things you started to do
From then what it's leadin' up to
Clues after clues and hints after hints.

©2016 Albert Cloudy. All rights reserved. Used with permission.

∆∆∆∆∆   *Focus on the Lift*   ∆∆∆∆∆

Intuition about next steps and possible outcomes… been thinking about this idea. Today has been interesting… day after leg day in the gym is always… let's say it this way… thought-provoking. Soooooo while working out today, I started thinking about the concept of mindset… state of mind… when you are working to take the next step in your goal journey. A few questions came to mind: Do you have a tangible goal? Have you prayed about what we could refer to as a "spiritual flowchart" for progressing toward your God-directed goal line? What is your mindset today? What was it yesterday? Will it be tomorrow? Sometimes, when we are reaching for a new level... trying to take that next step... we might think of excuses or reasons why we "can't"... but when we actually try... we often find that we Can Do It! Come on... Let's go get those goals. I know you can do it. Pray with me to understand the proper mindset, direction, and how we can invite Jesus to join us on our journey into a life built with trust and deeper relationships.

***

In or out of the zone...
"When You said, 'Seek My face,' my heart said to You,
'Your face, O LORD, I shall seek.'" (Psalm 27:8)
Invite the Holy Spirit to fill you and keep seeking the Lord's face. He will reveal His presence to you through people you meet, circumstances which enter your life, opportunities that come your way, scriptures that cross your path, and "difference-making" ideas that come to mind. Realize though, that God pulls you out of your comfort zone when He is calling you to follow Him. Remember that "God does not call the qualified. He qualifies the called." [Author unknown]

Question: Are you willing to get out of your comfort zone? Yes? Because that is where the Holy Spirit is going to meet you.

Remember, He is the Master Potter. We are His clay...

We are all earthen vessels to be filled with God's treasures... His Spirit, love, hope, gifts, and fruits. As God creates and fashions us, He has an intended purpose for our lives here on earth. If you have ever worked with clay, you know that when trying to mold and sculpt the clay, there will be some grit that needs to be discarded, and the clay may not "behave" according to your expectations, i.e., it may resist or oppose your efforts to form the material into the shape you envision. As we are the clay and God is the potter, do we sometimes (or often) resist His plans for us? Intentionally? Unintentionally?

By intentional, I am referring to those times when you recognize that "nudge," i.e., times when God is calling you to use the gifts He has given you to help carry out His will, and you ignore that feeling. He will fill us with His grace if we will welcome Him into our lives. Ask God to help you realize His presence in your life. Release yourself and refrain from putting up resistance to His leadings. You will begin to discern direction during times of uncertainty… times when you know that you want to find the treasures God has in store for you… to be placed into your earthly vessel where God is shaping you: the clay.

Filling your earthen vessel…

What exactly is an earthen vessel? When investigating this question, many publicly available information sources refer to Biblical references. Per Merriam Webster dictionary definitions of earthen and then of vessel, one learns that this combined phrase literally means a container composed of materials found within the planet earth's terrain.[8] So, we could list a myriad of substances such as, granite, iron, sandstone, onyx, clay… and the list continues. Scripturally speaking, we are earthen vessels, created by God, to be filled with His treasures.

When we allow the primal sustenance in everyday life to become our aim, rather than focus on running with endurance the race God has placed before us, our hearts can become displaced and we lose sight of the treasures stored for us in heaven. And, as declared in Hebrews 12:1-2, we operate daily within a "cloud of witnesses" where we are accountable for our actions. Others will see whether we are walking in the light of Christ, or if we are straying from the path. How do we react when we encounter rocks and potential stumbling blocks along the way in our lives? Remember, we learn in Philippians 4:6-7: "Be anxious for nothing, but in everything by prayer and supplication with thanksgiving let your requests be made known to God. And the peace of God, which surpasses all comprehension, will guard your hearts and your minds in Christ Jesus." Ask the Lord to share inspiration with you on how to be faith-filled, grace-filled, and spirit-filled each day. I have a true story on this thought to share with you.

The other day, I was thinking about working on a new clay sculpture idea. The beauty of the cephalopod, Nautilus, (which is currently becoming endangered because of poaching for sale of their beautiful shells, with its colors, stripes, and chambers), inspires me to think beyond my own proximity. This beautiful sea creature, like so many animals, strives each day to find sustenance and survive enemy attacks. Similar to our own daily journeys – physical, mental, and spiritual. From my perspective, the nautilus has a capacious appearance with its ever-widening spiral shell. Are we capacious? Yearning for our earthen vessel to be filled and overflow with the Holy Spirit? And, do we call upon the Holy Spirit to join us on our journey of perseverance in our lives? Spiritual battles break out along the path… requiring us to make choices over temptations, deceptions, and accusations, that could lead us astray. We have the liberty to make choices. We need to pray about our choices and ask for discernment regarding distractions from God's leadings. Seek His guidance along the way. Seek the treasure God has prepared for us. Seek to be filled with His loving presence.

God renews and restores us. Then, we need to release evidence of His works within us; that is, share His gifts and allow Him to bear fruit through us; thus, helping to grow His kingdom. As we seek renewal, we also need to ask God to remove the veil that obscures our true vision of Him.

"But to this day whenever Moses is read, a veil lies over their heart; but whenever a person turns to the Lord, the veil is taken away. Now the Lord is the Spirit, and where the Spirit of the Lord is, *there* is liberty. But we all, with unveiled face, beholding as in a mirror the glory of the Lord, are being transformed into the same image from glory to glory, just as from the Lord, the Spirit." (2Corinthians 3:15-18)

"And, know that as the veil is removed and we invite Jesus into our lives…'and you will know the truth, and the truth will make you free.'"(John 8:32)

Then, upon this awakening, we are called to be disciples:

2Corinthians 4: 6-18 teaches us:

For God, who said, "Light shall shine out of darkness," is the One who has shone in our hearts to give the Light of the knowledge of the glory of God in the face of Christ. But we have this treasure in earthen vessels, so that the surpassing greatness of the power will be of God and not from ourselves; *we are* afflicted in every way, but not crushed; perplexed, but not despairing; persecuted, but not forsaken; struck down, but not destroyed; always carrying about in the body the dying of Jesus, so that the life of Jesus also may be manifested in our body. For we who live are constantly being delivered over to death for Jesus' sake, so that the life of Jesus also may be manifested in our mortal flesh. So death works in us, but life in you. But having the same spirit of faith, according to what is written, "I BELIEVED, THEREFORE I SPOKE," we also believe, therefore we also speak, knowing that He who raised the Lord Jesus will raise us also with Jesus and will present us with you. For all things *are* for your sakes, so that the grace which is spreading to more and more people may cause the giving of thanks to abound to the glory of God. Therefore we do not lose heart, but though our outer man is decaying, yet our inner man is being renewed day by day. For momentary, light affliction is producing for us an eternal weight of glory far beyond all comparison, while we look not at the things which are seen, but at the things which are not seen; for the things which are seen are temporal, but the things which are not seen are eternal. (2Corinthians 4: 6-18)

As we continue to work through our own *Titanium Transformation*, while we learn how to strengthen relationships – vertically with God and horizontally with people – we come to recognize the message promulgated within the above verses in 2Corinthians 4. Paul continues to advise us: we need to give ourselves completely to the Lord, our God… love Him with all of our heart, soul, mind, and body.

Jesus' calling and our calling… to run the race for which God has prepared us…

Jesus spoke these things; and lifting up His eyes to heaven, He said, "Father, the hour has come; glorify Your Son, that the Son may glorify You, even as You gave Him authority over all flesh, that to all whom You have given Him, He may give eternal life. This is eternal life, that they may know You, the only true God, and Jesus Christ whom You have sent. I glorified You on the earth, having accomplished the work which You have given Me to do. Now, Father, glorify Me together with Yourself, with the glory which I had with You before the world was.

"I have manifested Your name to the men whom You gave Me out of the world; they were Yours and You gave them to Me, and they have kept Your word. Now they have come to know that everything You have given Me is from You; for the words which You gave Me I have given to them; and they received *them* and truly understood that I came forth from You, and they believed that You sent Me. I ask on their behalf; I do not ask on behalf of the world, but of those whom You have given Me; for they are Yours; and all things that are Mine are Yours, and Yours are Mine; and I have been glorified in them. I am no longer in the world; and *yet* they themselves are in the world, and I come to You. Holy Father, keep them in Your name, *the name* which You have given Me, that they may be one even as We *are*. While I was with them, I was keeping them in Your name which You have given Me; and I guarded them and not one of them perished but the son of perdition, so that the Scripture would be fulfilled." (John 17:1-12)

The poem, *The Chosen Vessel*,[9] by Beulah Cornwall, helps to further illustrate the idea that we are all clay awaiting the Master's work within us. Her poem brings to mind the following verses in 2 Timothy 2:20-26:

"Now in a large house there are not only gold and silver vessels, but also vessels of wood and of earthenware, and some to honor and some to dishonor. Therefore, if anyone cleanses himself from these *things*, he will be a vessel for honor, sanctified, useful to the Master, prepared for every good work. Now flee from youthful lusts and pursue righteousness, faith, love *and* peace, with those who call on the Lord from a pure heart. But refuse foolish and ignorant speculations, knowing that they produce quarrels. The Lord's bond-servant must not be quarrelsome, but be kind to all, able to teach, patient when wronged, with gentleness correcting those who are in opposition, if perhaps God may grant them repentance leading to the knowledge of the truth, and they may come to their senses *and escape* from the snare of the devil, having been held captive…"

Does your earthen vessel still have its integrity?

Integrity – inside and out? Is the dish still useful? For what purpose? Often, after a ceramic dish has been shattered and repaired, it will have a different function because adhesive repair materials are toxic and are not to be used near food. Much like ourselves after we have been brought through the fire… through a challenge in life. God brings us to a new path which often includes a discipleship role when we answer His call. We are called to not only receive God's treasures into our repaired earthen vessels, but also to go forth and share the Good News of our renewal, healing, and God's loving mercy with others.

The message…

Everyone has a story. Each of us has his/her own journey filled with joys and perils along the way. In my life story, at the time of the car wreck, I had forgotten that Jesus walks with me every day and carries me when I need Him to help me get over the rough spots in the road. I was trying to handle everything my way - not realizing that His way is so much more beautiful, effective, uplifting, and graceful. After escaping death on the highway and surviving a dozen surgeries during the following six years, I began to more fully recognize God's enduring love and presence in my life. He is here for us all. As we travel the path of life each day, let's try to see Christ in each moment of each day. He is there waiting for us to invite Him over the threshold and through the open door into our lives. Be not afraid and be anxious for nothing. Rely on Our Father and He will provide a light unto your path. Pray with me:

'Our Father who is in heaven,
Hallowed be Your name.
'Your kingdom come.
Your will be done,
On earth as it is in heaven.
'Give us this day our daily bread.
'And forgive us our debts, as we also have forgiven our debtors.
'And do not lead us into temptation, but deliver us from evil. [For Yours is the kingdom and the power and the glory forever. Amen.'] [Matthew 6:9-13]

A star in the sky…
How often do we share a moment of calmness with the Lord? God's presence is all around us and within us. And, His love is unconditional and beyond measure. He wants us to draw our strength from Him and invite Him into our awareness. Amazingly, when you seek a relationship with God, He helps you recognize His presence in your life. Does that reasoning seem circular? I assure you that it is not. As we further hone our skills of awareness of God's presence, we experience *Golden Moments* and our own increased responses to our G.P.S. (God's Presence Signal).

One day, our youngest daughter said, "Mama, I know why we saw that big bright star in the sky last night!" Her face was lit up with excitement and she could not wait to share her theory with me. I replied, "Why did we see it?" She then said, "That big bright star was God and He was showing us the way, just like He did for the shepherds who were trying to find Baby Jesus that night." Thought-provoking comment… God is trying to get our attention and show us the way. Are we aware enough to recognize His presence, i.e., His light, in our lives?

Ginny W. Frings, Ph.D.

You are meant to be…

One day, while in the midst of some career transitions and praying about how to proceed, I heard Steven Curtis Chapman's song from his CD entitled "Re-creation" [10] - knowing the story of the intense challenges which the Chapman family has survived – and then I began to listen to the message the Lord was sharing through Steven's music and lyrics. Wow! The song, "Meant to Be"[11] especially speaks to me, where the Lord tells us that all human encounters have a purpose… all smiles shared… all interactions… of all sizes… and "every move you make" has meaning. Interesting… I have moved sixteen times in my life. Looking back, it seems they occurred all within God's timing and planning. For example, my family was transferred from Atlanta to Birmingham during the summer before my senior year of high school. On the first day in my new school, I met my husband-to-be during homeroom. We are still together today. Let's embrace with open arms the opportunities that God places on our paths. Remember Matthew 19:26, where "And looking at them Jesus said to them, 'With people this is impossible, but with God all things are possible.'" Let's ask God to help us "make things possible" for others. We are meant to be here right now leading others with Christ-like forgiveness, mercy, and unconditional love. In a world where economic, relational, and political strife have become not just a developmental phase, but rather the norm, many people need help - spiritually, financially, socially, and occupationally. When taking some time to minister to others, you will reap bounty in your own life… now and eternally. Just like Steven sings, we are meant to be touching lives and we are here to be God's presence through our experiences and interactions within the lives of others. So, let's pray right now about those persons in our lives who need some forgiveness and compassion… someone to listen to them… a hug… or remember the free high fives story… yearning for something so simple as a "free high five" after a difficult day.

> "A candle is not dimmed by lighting another candle." [Author Unknown]

Reminders of perseverance…
I remember while recovering from the car wreck, being literally bandaged from head to toe, and then seeing the remaining scars as each injury healed and the bandages were removed. For those of us who have physical scars and for those of us who have emotional scars, what do we see when we look in the mirror? I had to learn that to Jesus, scars are "reminders of perseverance, rather than blemishes of tragedy."[12] Our experiences can prepare us to be a conduit for God's energy and presence to others. Let His light shine through you… outshining, healing, and looking beyond the scars. He invites you to share in life's joys with Him and He will be there for you when you need Him.

∆∆∆∆∆   *Focus on the Lift*   ∆∆∆∆∆

For this exercise, we will first describe challenges in our lives. Then, we will look at the changes needed to work though the problems, and finally place the experiences on a "spiritual potter's wheel" to mold them into a *cup of compassion* for others to know. One of my mottos is: "It is not <u>what</u> happens to you, but rather <u>what you do</u> with what happens to you." My father-in-law helped me craft that slogan during my recovery. He could see at the onset of my journey of physical and spiritual rehabilitation, that I would eventually share God's message of healing and encouragement with others who are searching for meaning in their lives. Compassion is a very important component of the spiritual journey, and so many people have shared their compassion for me and my family. When you are enduring difficult times in your own life, reaching out with compassion for another person can be hard… sometimes it feels impossible to feel compassion for someone else because you are either caught up in your own struggles or you are emerging from your challenges and have become calloused in the process. Having that "just get over it" attitude toward others is not God's way. Nor, is it the way in the gym. On a piece of paper, write down three challenges you are facing right now in your life. Then, write down three relationships that you feel are in need of strengthening. Next, refer back to your drawing of your clay cup of compassion. Fold your new page of lists and attach it (staple or tape) to your cup drawing. Now, take five minutes to ask Jesus to share your cup of compassion. Ask Him to show you how to better give and receive compassion and forgiveness. We are the cup (vessel) to be filled with the Lord's compassion. Pray with me: "Lord, we are the clay. You are the potter. Please mold us and fashion us into the image you envision."

***

Life is not about waiting for the storm to pass, but rather learning to dance in the rain. [Vivian Greene]

Sonshine…
Do you ever feel like there is rain on the horizon even when the skies are sunny and clear? Dark days can seemingly appear in our lives even on the summer solstice. And, then there appears a ray of Sonshine.

Here is the story where Jesus sent someone to share…

"She said to Him, 'Sir, You have nothing to draw with and the well is deep; where then do You get that living water?'

'You are not greater than our father Jacob, are You, who gave us the well, and drank of it himself and his sons and his cattle?'

Jesus answered and said to her, 'Everyone who drinks of this water will thirst again; but whoever drinks of the water that I will give him shall never thirst; but the water that I will give him will become in him a well of water springing up to eternal life.'" [John 4:11-14] Next, the woman left her bucket at the well when she went to tell others about Jesus at the well and share His life-giving message. We, too, are being called to share His word with others… His testimony… our testimony. Let's pray for understanding of this important calling to evangelize within your own *Titanium Transformation*.

Chapter 7

∞∞∞∞∞∞ **Understanding** ∞∞∞∞∞∞

Whenever we're afraid, it's because we don't know enough.
If we understood enough, we would never be afraid.
- Earl Nightingale

"How blessed is the man who finds wisdom
And the man who gains understanding." [Proverbs 3:13]

With each step we take…
Throughout the pages and exercises in this book so far, we have been learning how to strengthen ourselves both attitudinally and spiritually. And, while we have been sharpening our awareness of the Trinity's presence around and within ourselves, now it is time to take a closer look at our *Titanium Transformation* from the perspective of our relationships. It's time to do a 360 degree examination of how we interact with others.

Does that make sense…?
We teachers often ask that question to get a barometer reading on how well the students are understanding the lesson. But, actually we need to ask ourselves the same question when communicating and interacting with other people. Rather than judging each other, we can each seek to understand the other person's situation… perspective… path… background… goals… challenges… and then maybe he/she will "make more sense" to each of us.

Ginny W. Frings, Ph.D.

How to ask…

Do you ever remember being in a classroom, trying to take notes, and beginning to feel the frustration rise as you realize that you actually don't understand the lesson… or how to work the problems… and as your confidence is waning, you're not sure what question to ask… partly out of embarrassment? Ok… so it was AP Calculus for me… I'm here sweating as I write about that scenario! I'm not trying to dredge up unpleasant memories for anyone, but some people live with these same types of feelings every day. They need a friend… someone to talk with who will listen and not judge… someone who genuinely wants to understand their journey and daily struggles… someone to share stories with… cry with… laugh with… share a hug or high five with… someone who cares. But, they might not know how or what to ask in order for you to recognize their cry in need of a friend. Let's sit quietly for a few moments to read and reflect on Albert Cloudy's poem about understanding others.

UNDERSTANDING
by Albert Cloudy

If you only knew how it really is
Stop and take a step back
Unlace your shoes and slip on theirs
Enter a world you may not recognize
Something you are not used to and don't understand
Don't judge or to think too quick
To know a person you first have to understand
That they might be different than you
Maybe less fortunate than you but goes through life everyday
Trying to Pretend and blend in
May even have an abuser at home
Who hides the scars on the inside and the out
And smiles and seems happy
Who's crying on the inside that just won't come out
So before assumptions are made

Before you laugh and that person's face
Stop and take that step back
To think and be more understanding.

©2016 Albert Cloudy. All rights reserved. Used with permission.

Jesus understands…

Jesus knows each of us and He can relate to how we are trying to work through our struggles. He genuinely understands our brokenness and wants to help us see purpose in life. Jesus personifies faith in action. Let's read the following stories.

The Transfiguration

Six days later Jesus took with Him Peter and James and John his brother, and led them up on a high mountain by themselves.

And He was transfigured before them; and His face shone like the sun, and His garments became as white as light.

And behold, Moses and Elijah appeared to them, talking with Him.

Peter said to Jesus, "Lord, it is good for us to be here; if You wish, I will make three tabernacles here, one for You, and one for Moses, and one for Elijah."

While he was still speaking, a bright cloud overshadowed them, and behold, a voice out of the cloud said, "This is My beloved Son, with whom I am well-pleased; listen to Him!"

When the disciples heard this, they fell face down to the ground and were terrified.

And Jesus came to them and touched them and said, "Get up, and do not be afraid."

And lifting up their eyes, they saw no one except Jesus Himself alone.

As they were coming down from the mountain, Jesus commanded them, saying, "Tell the vision to no one until the Son of Man has risen from the dead."

And His disciples asked Him, "Why then do the scribes say that [K] Elijah must come first?"

And He answered and said, "Elijah is coming and will restore all things;

but I say to you that Elijah already came, and they did not recognize him, but did to him whatever they wished. So also the Son of Man is going to suffer at their hands."

Then the disciples understood that He had spoken to them about John the Baptist. [Matthew 17:1-13]

Another story…

The Demoniac

When they came to the crowd, a man came up to Jesus, falling on his knees before Him and saying,

"Lord, have mercy on my son, for he is a lunatic and is very ill; for he often falls into the fire and often into the water.

"I brought him to Your disciples, and they could not cure him."

And Jesus answered and said, "You unbelieving and perverted generation, how long shall I be with you? How long shall I put up with you? Bring him here to Me."

And Jesus rebuked him, and the demon came out of him, and the boy was cured at once.

Then the disciples came to Jesus privately and said, "Why could we not drive it out?"

And He said to them, "Because of the littleness of your faith; for truly I say to you, if you have faith the size of a mustard seed, you will say to this mountain, 'Move from here to there,' and it will move; and nothing will be impossible to you.

["But this kind does not go out except by prayer and fasting."]

And while they were gathering together in Galilee, Jesus said to them, "The Son of Man is going to be delivered into the hands of men;

And they will kill Him, and He will be raised on the third day." And they were deeply grieved. [Matthew 17:14-23]

The message that Jesus is sharing within these experiences is a testament to all of us for keeping our faith in God alive and strong. The more time we dedicate to spiritual growth and building our compassion for others, we will be leaning in to God's call to us.

ΔΔΔΔΔ   *Focus on the Lift*   ΔΔΔΔΔ

Here's a question for you: Do you consider yourself to be patient? Well, I admit that I am not very patient. But, in time many of us have come to learn to realize that achieving any goal... whether it be physical fitness... educational readiness... business development... or spiritual mindedness... requires discipline and patience... and faith! The journey to reach your goal may be filled with trying days... sleepless nights... moments of revelation... intermediate victories... inspired leaps... and yes... times of patience. When we recognize this reality, we then realize that we can do this. Jesus is extending His hand out to you. He wants to walk - and run - with you to the finish line! Ready. Set. Go. Jesus is waiting for you. Let's pray. Jesus, I am inviting you into my life and I am asking you to join me on my journey. Please carry me over the stormy seas, through the barren desert straights, and across the deep chasms, that I will encounter on my path. Thank you for always being there for me, Lord. Amen.

***

Pray with an attitude... say what?
Typically, when we say someone has "an attitude," it is not a very positive observation. But, when we look at scriptural references to "having an attitude," this phrase takes on a whole new meaning! Read the following verses for example:

> Philippians 2:5
> Have this attitude in yourselves which was also in Christ Jesus,

> Philippians 3:15
> Let us therefore, as many as are perfect, have this attitude; and if in anything you have a different attitude, God will reveal that also to you;

> Colossians 4:2
> Devote yourselves to prayer, keeping alert in it with an attitude of thanksgiving;

> James 2:1
> [The Sin of Partiality] My brethren, do not hold your faith in our glorious Lord Jesus Christ with an attitude of personal favoritism.

So, let's pray with an attitude of thanksgiving... with Christ's attitude of love... and with an attitude of unconditional trust. Take a moment to let this idea sink in...

Relax with Jesus, again...
Earlier, we talked about relaxing with Jesus. Now, we are going to just chill. What good is stressing over an uncontrollable situation going to

do for you – physically or emotionally? Rather, stress on the human body and mind can be detrimental. As we discussed earlier, we are learning to identify the "good" stresses and mitigate the "bad" stresses in our lives.

Luke 12:25 causes us to contemplate: "And which of you by worrying can add a *single* hour to his life's span?"

Put on your dancing shoes…
Here's a true story. One autumn day, I was getting ready for work and decided to wear my blue clogs (the pair of shoes was about thirteen years old but the navy blue suede still looked fairly new). So, I arrived at the university and parked in the faculty lot. As I was walking across campus, it felt as though my shoes were a little… how should I say… "springy" as I took each step. I arrived at my office and when I looked down at the floor, there were black pieces of something on the carpet. Then, I looked outside my office door and saw a trail of what looked to be this same material. I took off my clogs… oh my… the soles were disintegrating with each step I had taken. In five minutes, I had to be in the classroom to teach a class. So, I carefully walked to the classroom. While teaching that day, I did not walk around the room as much as usual. When class was over, I thought I could drive home to pick up another pair of shoes and then come back to campus before my next class. And, then it happened. My boss walked into my classroom as the students were packing up their belongings. She made a quick announcement about upcoming events to the students. Then, she tells me that she would like to talk with me in my office. *Oh no*, I am thinking. *This can't be good. And, on all days… when my shoes are falling apart.* So, we walk to my office… my boss is laughing about what's left of my clogs at this point and says, "Ginny, this is like following a trail of bread crumbs," as she chuckles. We arrive at my office and she walks through the door, closes the door, and begins to talk in hushed tones. At this point, my stress level is rising and I say, "Sandy, let's get to the point. Are you about to fire me?" She replies, "Oh no, Ginny, on the contrary. We put an instructor at an off-campus MBA site and now we

realize that we need someone with more experience to teach that course. We would like you to teach those students." I just start laughing. Sandy says, "What's so funny?" I say, "It's pretty ironic that the day that my shoes are literally falling apart is the same day that you are asking me to put my best foot forward for the university!" We both laugh.

Message from the story: When "not so great" or "embarrassing" things are happening in your life… just keep looking ahead… when you ask God to direct your life, He will do so and the changes will be glorious… in the midst of an embarrassing shoe-falling-apart day, I was being asked to represent the university in a very public and mind-shaping role. God has a sense of humor and when He is working out His plan, even deteriorating shoes that may be distracting to us, are not distracting to His messengers (Sandy) – she thought it was cute. And, I had so much fun teaching the course that semester.

> A time to weep and a time to laugh; A time to mourn and a time to dance. [Ecclesiastes 3:4]

On a rainy day…
Do you ever spend a few moments just listening to the sounds of raindrops splashing on your roof… batting against the windows… or cascading down onto a skylight during a rain storm? Have you ever heard the sound of rain falling onto a tin roof? I remember having that experience while visiting my grandparents' house on summer afternoons as a child. Rainwater has cleansing properties and is necessary for photosynthesis and our own sustainability. A few days ago, the children and I were out running errands during some scattered rainstorms. When we had finished our last errand for the day, we walked out of the store and a most beautiful rainbow greeted us in the evening sky. The rain had paused, and the sun was beginning to set. The sky was absolutely breathtaking in the splendor of sunset colors and decorated with a rainbow. The sky was bright and the air was still moist from the rain… creating a cleansing feeling.

In life's rainstorms, God is our umbrella…
We all experience times in our lives when we feel like we are working to survive and weather a thunder storm, where the lightning is crashing to the ground and we are seeking a place of safety… a safe harbor. Where is your safe harbor? Jesus invites us to seek safety with Him. He will shield us from the pelting rain. Thomas Merton, poet and author, said "Be good, keep your feet dry, your eyes open, your heart at peace and your soul in the joy of Christ."

"Hit it"…
Have any of you ever waterskied in the rain? Before we owned a boat, we accepted occasional invitations to go waterskiing with family and friends. And, there were many times when we were slalom skiing behind the boat at 38 knots and the raindrops were stinging during a brief storm. But, it was worth it just to feel the spray on our faces as we made the jumps and cuts. I think we can all relate on some level. Are there risks you take during "storms," whether physically… finishing the eighteenth hole on that Friday afternoon during an approaching thunderstorm… reeling in one more fish as the lightning is striking in the distance… or figuratively… taking chances with occupational… educational… familial… or relational… experiences where the result could go sideways? Many members of the world's population have expressed their fears about the unknown and their concerns about the risks of war, political leaders' agendas, economic trends, and what the future holds. Conditions of our planet are exhibiting indicators that we read about in the Book of Revelations… hmmm… think about the parallels.

Dancing in the rain…
Have you ever had an unexpected opportunity for an outdoor activity and then it rained? I think we all have! Here is a true story. One day, while living in Dunwoody, Georgia, it was summer break from school and my older sister, Gail, was visiting. I wanted to take her to the club to play some tennis (all in fun, but let's just say we are a little competitive when it comes to sports), so we went and began to play. That day, the

sets were pretty even and then… a southern summer afternoon rain came pouring down on us. Did we run for cover? No. Instead, we kept playing and had one of the most enjoyable afternoons! The soggy tennis balls began bouncing a little lower after awhile. Finally, we decided to go home. Then, we remembered that we had to walk through the pro shop to get back to the car. Oh, the looks we received as we, the two drenched tennis players who, in others' opinions, "did not have sense enough to get out of the rain," walked through the club pro shop. We were the ones giggling as they stared at us. My sister and I had enjoyed a delightful afternoon. Next, we went home, dried off, and told the family about our beautiful outing… dancing around the tennis court in the rain. By the way, Sis,… who won the match that day? So, adaptation to change, and inviting the Holy Spirit into our lives, while looking to God and His Son for direction, are imperative for experiencing *silent reassurance*[1] and living a spirit-filled life… yes… even on rainy days.

ΔΔΔΔΔ   *Focus on the Lift*   ΔΔΔΔΔ

Let's look at the Cross picture that we drew in Chapter 2. Take a few moments to pray about any recent "rainy set" day (literally or figuratively) circumstances and your responses to the challenges before you on those days. Write down those experiences and attach them to the base of your Cross picture. Then, ask God to help you respond in the manner to which He calls you during future storms.

***

1-2-3…1-2-3…
Think about the many styles of dance: ballet, tap, folk, square, cha cha, salsa, bachata … jazz, disco, jitterbug, Latin, polka, ballroom, Irish, clogging, cardio hip hop, flamenco. break… and the list continues.

We've all heard the phrase, "It takes two to tango." Now, let's add some more alliteration as we focus on a new perspective on the role of relationships in our *Titanium Transformation*. We can "salsa with strength" and "bachata with breath" and "flamenco with faith"... you get the idea.

ΔΔΔΔΔ *Focus on the Lift* ΔΔΔΔΔ

Tango with tenacity...
Persevere in your "life dance" seeking to follow God's path for your life. I remember when disco was popular and I ordered a disco album (yes, an album to play on my record player) and it came with a paper "map" of the steps in the form of outlined footprints and arrows. So, I turned on the music and then began to try to move to the rhythm while working to follow the arrows and step on the appropriate sequence of footprints... good thing no video cameras were rolling! Thinking back on that experience, it resembles the conversations I have with God asking Him to direct my steps and carry me through situations where I do not know how to follow His "arrows," i.e., I do not see the path. For this exercise, you will need three sheets of paper. On the first sheet, write the heading "Tango with tenacity...following God's lead." Then, below that phrase on that sheet, write one sentence about a goal you are trying to achieve or a challenge you are trying to work through. Then, pray to God and His Son, and ask Them to "take the lead" in your life. They will direct your steps and guide you to completion of the tasks you have listed. Ask Them to intervene in your life and sharpen your awareness of Their presence. Repeat this exercise on two more sheets by writing the headings: "Flamenco with faith... in step with Jesus" and "Bachata with breath... of the Holy Spirit." Then, each day, draw outlines of footprints and describe the people, places, things, and ideas that cross your daily path, which may be part of God's plan... working to hone your awareness and responses to His leadings.

***

From questions to quenching…

Throughout the seasons of our lives, we all experience situations where we question the reasoning why certain events are occurring… whether it's the timing, or the event, itself. Here's an example from Exodus where the followers were angry with Moses for leading them into a parched wilderness. See what happens next…

"Then Moses led Israel from the Red Sea, and they went out into the wilderness of Shur; and they went three days in the wilderness and found no water.

When they came to Marah, they could not drink the waters of Marah, for they were bitter; therefore it was named Marah.

So the people grumbled at Moses, saying, "What shall we drink?"

Then he cried out to the LORD, and the LORD showed him a tree; and he threw it into the waters, and the waters became sweet There He made for them a statute and regulation, and there He tested them.

And He said, "If you will give earnest heed to the voice of the LORD your God, and do what is right in His sight, and give ear to His commandments, and keep all His statutes, I will put none of the diseases on you which I have put on the Egyptians; for I, the LORD, am your healer."

Then they came to Elim where there were twelve springs of water and seventy date palms, and they camped there beside the waters." [Exodus 15:22-27]

Moses deeply believed and had unconditional faith that God was ever-present and traveling with him and his followers. God gives grace. He is grace. Let's invite Him into our journey.

△△△△△ *Focus on the Lift* △△△△△

Dear God, Jesus, and Holy Spirit…
Write your invitation to the Trinity to join you in your life's journey. They are extraordinary traveling companions. Prayerfully dialogue with Them and experience Their presence. You are gaining a deeper understanding of how to live life with Christ at the center.

***

Learning through stories told by the masterful storyteller… Jesus…
In Matthew 13, we feel as though we have entered Jesus' classroom as we travel and witness in the presence of the disciples. Jesus teaches us through parables. Let's step away from the rush of everyday life and relax with Jesus while He shares these life-giving messages. Let's read each of the following parables and then we will prayerfully discern lessons and guidance for our lives and how to build stronger relationships.

Jesus Teaches in Parables

That day Jesus went out of the house and was sitting by the sea.

And large crowds gathered to Him, so He got into a boat and sat down, and the whole crowd was standing on the beach.

The Sower

And He spoke many things to them in parables, saying, "Behold, the sower went out to sow;

and as he sowed, some seeds fell beside the road, and the birds came and ate them up.

"Others fell on the rocky places, where they did not have much soil; and immediately they sprang up, because they had no depth of soil.

"But when the sun had risen, they were scorched; and because they had no root, they withered away.

"Others fell among the thorns, and the thorns came up and choked them out.

"And others fell on the good soil and yielded a crop, some a hundredfold, some sixty, and some thirty.

"He who has ears, let him hear." [Matthew 13:1-9]

"But blessed are your eyes, because they see; and your ears, because they hear.

"For truly I say to you that many prophets and righteous men desired to see what you see, and did not see it, and to hear what you hear, and did not hear it.

The Sower Explained

"Hear then the parable of the sower.

"When anyone hears the word of the kingdom and does not understand it, the evil one comes and snatches away what has been sown in his heart. This is the one on whom seed was sown beside the road.

"The one on whom seed was sown on the rocky places, this is the man who hears the word and immediately receives it with joy;

yet he has no firm root in himself, but is only temporary, and when affliction or persecution arises because of the word, immediately he falls away.

"And the one on whom seed was sown among the thorns, this is the man who hears the word, and the worry of the world and the deceitfulness of wealth choke the word, and it becomes unfruitful.

"And the one on whom seed was sown on the good soil, this is the man who hears the word and understands it; who indeed bears fruit and brings forth, some a hundredfold, some sixty, and some thirty." [Matthew 13:16-23]

Question for you: What type of soil are you?

The Mustard Seed

He presented another parable to them, saying, "The kingdom of heaven is like a mustard seed, which a man took and sowed in his field;

and this is smaller than all other seeds, but when it is full grown, it is larger than the garden plants and becomes a tree, so that THE BIRDS OF THE AIR come and NEST IN ITS BRANCHES." [Matthew 13:31-32]

Question for you: In this parable, Jesus teaches that we can plant the seed of faith, although ever so small, and if we tend the garden of our lives with life-giving water and sunshine (Sonshine), God will help us reap a strong and beautiful bounty. Is there a seed of faith taking root within you? How are you nourishing its growth?

Jesus continues…

"Have you understood all these things?" They said to Him, "Yes."

And Jesus said to them, "Therefore every scribe who has become a disciple of the kingdom of heaven is like a head of a household, who brings out of his treasure things new and old."

Jesus Revisits Nazareth

When Jesus had finished these parables, He departed from there.

He came to His hometown and began teaching them in their synagogue, so that they were astonished, and said, "Where did this man get this wisdom and these miraculous powers?

"Is not this the carpenter's son? Is not His mother called Mary, and His brothers, James and Joseph and Simon and Judas?

"And His sisters, are they not all with us? Where then did this man get all these things?"

And they took offense at Him But Jesus said to them, "A prophet is not without honor except in his hometown and in his own household."

And He did not do many miracles there because of their unbelief. [Matthew 13:51-58]

\ΔΔΔΔΔ   *Focus on the Lift*   ΔΔΔΔΔ

Let's read this verse, again: "And Jesus said to them, 'Therefore every scribe who has become a disciple of the kingdom of heaven is like a head of a household, who brings out of his treasure things new and old.'" [Matthew 13:52] Now, think about your role within God's kingdom. To continue building relationships within your *Titanium Transformation* process, we need to recognize that Jesus is teaching us, through His use of parable pedagogy, about our responsibilities as His disciples. And, He notes that His father has equipped us with the treasure necessary to lift up others along the way, as we strive to carry out God's will within our lives. So, on a piece of paper, write down five traits that you feel have been given to you from God which will, when honed, be ingredients of your treasure to share with others whom you meet on your journey. Next, ask Jesus how you should exercise those traits for strength - kind of like resistance training. He could call on you to add some weight to the barbell when learning how to lift up situations and events to Him for direction. Sit quietly for a little while. Write down the feelings and nudges you are experiencing. Then, walk through the following days with a renewed spirit of awareness… seeking cognizance about His responses to your questions… even through the words and actions of others around you. Make note of these experiences as Jesus walks the road with you.

***

Compassion and Stewardship…
As you continue to work through the previous *Focus on the Lift* exercise, we will revisit the roles that compassion and stewardship play within our lives. Read this story about Jesus' heartfelt compassion for a grieving mother…

"Soon afterwards He went to a city called Nain; and His disciples were going along with Him, accompanied by a large crowd. Now as He approached the gate of the city, a dead man was being carried out, the only son of his mother, and she was a widow; and a sizeable crowd from the city was with her. When the Lord saw her, He felt compassion for her, and said to her, "Do not weep." And He came up and touched the coffin; and the bearers came to a halt. And He said, "Young man, I say to you, arise!" The dead man sat up and began to speak. And Jesus gave him back to his mother. Fear gripped them all, and they began glorifying God, saying, "A great prophet has arisen among us!" and, "God has visited His people!" This report concerning Him went out all over Judea and in all the surrounding district." [Luke 7:11-17]

So, Jesus illustrates evidence of the importance of sowing, tending, and reaping seeds of compassion to make a difference in others' lives. He is preparing us for the harvest.

Stewardship – caring for and thinking of others…
Now, it's time to add another ingredient to our strength building process. Remember, we have completed exercises focusing on relationships and communication. The Capstone of this entire *Titanium Transformation* process, taught throughout this book, is that we must become acutely aware of God's grace in our lives. Paul emphasizes this reality during his teaching in Ephesians 3. Read these verses with me.

"For this reason I, Paul, the prisoner of Christ Jesus for the sake of you Gentiles-- if indeed you have heard of the stewardship of God's grace which was given to me for you; that by revelation there was made known to me the mystery, as I wrote before in brief. By referring to this, when you read you can understand my insight into the mystery of Christ, which in other generations was not made known to the sons of men, as it has now been revealed to His holy apostles and prophets in the Spirit; to be specific, that the Gentiles are fellow heirs and fellow members of the body, and fellow partakers of the promise in Christ Jesus through the gospel, of which I was made a minister, according to the gift of God's grace which was given to me according to the working of His power. To me, the very least of all saints, this grace was given, to preach to the Gentiles the unfathomable riches of Christ, and to bring to light what is the administration of the mystery which for ages has been hidden in God who created all things; so that the manifold wisdom of God might now be made known through the church to the rulers and the authorities in the heavenly places. This was in accordance with the eternal purpose which He carried out in Christ Jesus our Lord, in whom we have boldness and confident access through faith in Him." [Ephesians 3:1-12]

"Now to Him who is able to do far more abundantly beyond all that we ask or think, according to the power that works within us, to Him be the glory in the church and in Christ Jesus to all generations forever and ever. Amen." [Ephesians 3:20-21]

ΔΔΔΔΔ   *Focus on the Lift*   ΔΔΔΔΔ

This exercise involves thinking of others. The Commandment to "love one another…" includes encouraging each other. Let's live this Commandment today: at least five times today, give someone words of encouragement, either spoken, written, or communicated in some way that is meaningful to the other person… could even be a real "high five" and a smile! When the other person smiles back at you, how does that make you feel? Pretty good, huh… when we show Christ's love to others, it comes back to us multiplied. After each "sharing a high five" experience, write a few lines about the happening – who, scenario, how they reacted, and how it made you feel. You will come away from this exercise with increased understanding of how a little compassion can help others work through their challenges… even more than you realize.

***

Ok, so you have progressed through the first seven steps within your *Titanium Transformation* process. Now, it's time to dive into the Meaning behind this method of building a stronger you whilst strengthening surrounding relationships.

Chapter 8
∞∞∞∞∞∞ Meaning ∞∞∞∞∞∞

As Mother Teresa said, "A life not lived for others is not worthwhile."

Here are some thoughts on "meaning" as seen through the eyes of the young poet, Albert Cloudy.

MEANING
by Albert Cloudy

Something I care for the most
The feeling that I receive when I have it
It must mean something
What's Intended to be
Now I understand why
What it means to have meaning
Something you can't live without
Constant Reminder wherever you go
That loss of breath by just the thought
It's a signal that, That Person, Place, or thing
Means something significant to you
That it has meaning.

©2016 Albert Cloudy. All rights reserved. Used with permission.

Live your life with Consistency and Purpose…
So far in *U R Titanium*, we have focused on building strength and compassion into your relationships – horizontally with others and vertically with God. And, we have practiced with exercises on dialoguing with others and with God. Effective communication between the parties in a relationship is imperative for positive growth. In this chapter, we will weave it all together into a fabric of *Titanium Transformation* where the *armor's chainmail* of your relationships are connected with God as the center link. Think about that idea… quite a Majestic image…

∆∆∆∆∆   *Focus on the Lift*   ∆∆∆∆∆

In this exercise, we will be activating the scriptural elements of the Armor of God into our own lives. To review, Ephesians 6 describes the parts of this armor: helmet of salvation, breastplate of justice, belt of truth, footgear of the zeal to spread God's word and gospel, shield of faith, and sword of God's word and spirit. For three days, write down the ways in which you shared each piece of your armor with someone else – through words and/or actions. For example, when have you brought the shield of faith to life for someone because you took the time to encourage and pray with him/her in the midst of a challenge he/she is facing… helping that person to have hope and the beginnings of a renewed spirit in Christ?

You are being called to come alive and live your life with Consistency and Purpose.

"And we know that God causes all things to work together for good to those who love God, to those who are called according to His purpose." [Romans 8:28]

***

Ginny W. Frings, Ph.D.

Task clarification: Lifting the veil of fog…
Are there days when you feel like you can't find direction, i.e., it seems as though you are out at sea and the lighthouse is hidden… either the waves are too high and your boat is being thrown about… or you look to the horizon and feel as though you are not in sight of land…i.e., not able to "see the light"? We all have life experiences where changes occur that we do not understand and many of us do not realize that we can ask God and His Son to guide us to safety. And, not only that, but They are on call and available to respond to our distress call… our S.O.S.… every day of the year… 24/7.

God is trying to reach out to us, His children. He is sharing His vision of building a bridge across the turbulent waters in our lives and guiding us to safety, while filling us with His grace and placing people in our lives… each with a specific purpose and role in our life path. Jesus is our everlasting light. Allow Him to shine his life-giving light into your life… shining on you and through you for others to see.

WWJD? Ask Him…He will answer…
I recently saw a license plate that read: WWJD ASK. Think about that question and answer. Circumstances can lead us to question why we are moving in a certain direction and why challenges sometimes seem like fog so dense we cannot see the stepping stones on the path in front of us. God sent us a ray of sun – His Son - to break through the fog that obstructs our view of Him. With fog on the horizon, it can skew our perception of God's direction. Warm air meeting cooler air tends to create foggy conditions, and then wind currents transport the fog along a particular path. Interestingly, God can allow the "winds of change" to blow causing us to look up from what we are doing and seek guidance. When the wind blows and the fog rolls in, what do you do? Turn on your fog lights? Do those ever really help? How about stepping back from your earthly toil for a moment and inviting God's Son into your life. The lighthouse of Jesus can cut through the fog and He can help you see the course you need to follow. Then, you can pursue a workable solution with a clear view. When you find yourself in a fog, let Him lift you up and **F**ocus **O**n **G**od.

I think we all have questions, especially during times of change. What changes are you dealing with? Does it seem like intended solutions are faltering? Are doors closing? Is there fog obscuring your view of the horizon? Next, let's learn how to let God clear that fog, shed His light, share His timing, and show us His meaning. Isaiah describes this thought:

"No longer will you have the sun for light by day,
Nor for brightness will the moon give you light;
But you will have the LORD for an everlasting light,
And your God for your glory." [Isaiah 60:19]

Proverbs 16:3 advises us to entrust our works to the Lord and our plans will succeed. When we focus on God, He will lift the veil of fog that is keeping us from seeing the plans He has for us. Whose initiatives are we working on – our internal temporal plans or His eternal? It seems to me that we can become myopic when trying to set goals and overall objectives for our lives. God can help us bridge the gap between where we are today and where we want to be; i.e., where He wants us to be. We are invited to live in His love and receive His grace on a daily basis. Ask the Lord, your God, to lead your life and He will do that, while He teaches you some powerful leadership skills in the process. He asks us to evangelize and disciple while living a life of prayerful connection with Him. Does that sound difficult? In Galatians, we learn about bearing one another's burdens and finding the strength to persevere.

"Brethren, even if anyone is caught in any trespass, you who are spiritual, restore such a one in a spirit of gentleness; *each one* looking to yourself, so that you too will not be tempted. Bear one another's burdens, and thereby fulfill the law of Christ. For if anyone thinks he is something when he is nothing, he deceives himself. But each one must examine his own work, and then he will have *reason for* boasting in regard to himself alone, and not in regard to another. For each one will bear his own load.

The one who is taught the word is to share all good things with the one who teaches *him*. Do not be deceived, God is not mocked; for whatever a man sows, this he will also reap. For the one who sows to his own flesh will from the flesh reap corruption, but the one who sows to the Spirit will from the Spirit reap eternal life. Let us not lose heart in doing good, for in due time we will reap if we do not grow weary. So then, while we have opportunity, let us do good to all people, and especially to those who are of the household of the faith." [Galatians 6:1-10]

∆∆∆∆∆ *Focus on the Lift* ∆∆∆∆∆

While studying the scripture quoted above, the image that comes to mind, for me, is one of a relay race where the runners take turns carrying the torch… handing it off to the next person at the appropriate time. Just like a relay race, life requires teamwork and cooperation each day to help each of us arrive at the next milestone in our own journey. As we work on building stronger relationships, let's think about how we can better focus on effectively engaging and communicating with others, so that we all make progress toward reaching the goal line. When training for fitness, we talk about having S.M.A.R.T. goals where S stands for specific; M is measurable; A is attainable; R is realistic; and T is timely. Refer back to your Personal Mission Statement exercise from Chapter 2. Let's pray for discipline to stay on point…the decision to focus on the next step… and delight when reaching each milestone. Commitment is key. Come on… it's time to commit to a strategy for achieving your S.M.A.R.T. goals. Let's do this. Jesus is your teammate in reaching your S.M.A.R.T. goals.

***

Every little thing you do…
Do you ever wonder if all of the seemingly "little" tasks you do each day are important? Do they really matter to anyone? In the business world, we analyze activities and projects to see if they "add value" to

the company. If not, then we scrap those projects and invest our limited resources into initiatives that will make an immediate difference in the sustainable solvency of the company. So, back to my question - what about the "little" things we do each day for people around us – are they "value-added"... in our lives... in the lives of others? Yes, indeed they are! Steven Curtis Chapman shares mighty insights into this conundrum that we all face when he sings his song entitled "Do Everything"[1] – where every little thing you do matters as long as you do it all in the name of God, i.e., sharing His love and caring ways with others in your life. God appreciates what we do in His name and in service to Him. Let's take a moment right now to thank God for giving meaning to our lives and ask Him to help us to see His presence more clearly.

More about adding value within each other's lives...
Sometimes, we get so laser focused on carrying out day to day "activities," that we ignore the daily "productivity" schedule that we could be experiencing for God's everlasting kingdom. This concept is interesting – productivity versus activity. When I teach classes about business production cycles, we discuss the differences between the costs of "activity" versus the costs of "productivity." In a business, we question whether particular processes are value-added and do they actually contribute to the success of the company. What are the upstream (planning, research, design) in contrast to downstream (implementation, distribution, service) costs which every organization faces? As we apply these concepts to our own lives and initiatives, think about who is leading your "life production cycle"? What are your daily inputs, processes, and outputs? What is the current state of your spiritual walk? Desired future state? Expectations by you and others? These questions are deep and are not to be answered without some spiritual reflection and dialogue with God. Take some time right now to prayerfully reach out for direction when responding to those questions. For those of you familiar with business outsourcing, take this exercise a step further and consider the vertically integrated and horizontally integrated aspects of your life – spiritually, personally, professionally. Something to think and pray about...

Ginny W. Frings, Ph.D.

ΔΔΔΔΔ *Focus on the Lift* ΔΔΔΔΔ

Weaving together the threads of our relationships...
So, when we take the time to review… analyze… investigate… or make note of… our daily productivity in the realm of relational efficiency and effectiveness, we begin to recognize with more clarity how our interactions with others affect how we achieve our goals. To put it another way, we can glean greater understanding of the meaning of people in our lives, and though possibly once ignored, we now see value in pruning and growing those relationships. In this exercise, you are striving to identify particular characteristics of your connections with others in your life, so that you can then determine which characteristics to prune away and which ones to fertilize and water, i.e., encourage to grow. On a piece of paper, write two columns:

<u>Relationship description</u>   <u>Three main characteristics</u>

Then, list at least ten connections you have with other people… legitimate relationships where you are truly friends with this person, or see this person or talk with this person on a regular basis, or are blood relatives. Next, list three main characteristics that you feel define your relationship with each person. For example, peer, leader, mentor, parent, child, friend, teacher, student, pleasant, hard, joyful, dread, love, hate, inviting, fearful, inspirational, intimidating, energizing, depleting, etc.

Now, it's time to ask Jesus to help you properly categorize these relationships where they will enhance spiritual growth for you and the others who play a role in your life. Consider His journey here within the human condition with its' emotions, distractions, and troubles… yet, He became and still becomes the light into so many lives. His mercy endures forever.

***

To the moon and back...
The world is continually experiencing change on many facets: political, economic, technological, defense... and with the world operating at the "speed of life," we need to be flexible in our thinking, attitudes, and openness to new ideas and process improvements. From a universal perspective, astronomers study changes in planet surfaces... and, now they only recognize eight spheres in our solar system as planets, instead of nine. Yes, the old cliché is true: Change is inevitable.

So, why do we resist change? Rather, how can we embrace it? Remember, my father-in-law helped me write my motivational programs slogan: "It's not *what* happens to you, but rather *what you do* with what happens to you," as he began to mentor me in the art of becoming an effective motivational speaker. When obstacles occur in our lives, instead of dwelling on the situation, let's ask God to help us look to the other side and reach out for what we will be able to *do* with the experience, once we arrive at a solution. God knows that we are human and we sometimes get so wrapped up in life's earthly events that we forget to "look up" and "look out" to feel His presence. Just as we practiced in *Navigate with God,*² let's practice being aware of God's presence in our lives. Invite Him into the conversation, completely and uncensored. He will help you work through the changes, clean-up the messes, repair the brokenness, and seek the joy.

ΔΔΔΔΔ *Focus on the Lift* ΔΔΔΔΔ

Some days seem to bring about a few reality checks... yes.. you can relate? Updates on projects... next steps outlined and scheduled... prayerful perspectives in place... teamwork... timing... and transitions. Changes and challenges in our lives can cause us to look up from our busy-ness long enough to take a deep breath and then realize that others are working through difficult times as well. In the Bible, we read that where two or more are gathered in the name of Christ, He will be there with them. So, let's reach out with compassion to people near us and together gather the Courage to work through the rough spots... the Confidence to know that we can do this... and the Can-do attitude to reach for our goals. Invite the Holy Spirit into this exercise and pray for awareness of the leadings.

∗∗∗

Sustenance for spiritual workout…
When we are planning to work out, whether physically, mentally, or spiritually, we must prepare, i.e., "eat and hydrate," before engaging in the fitness routine. Nourishing ourselves takes on different meanings depending upon the type of workout we are preparing to do. That said, think about the following scriptures where Jesus talks of spiritual sustenance.

"I am the living bread that came down out of heaven; if anyone eats of this bread, he will live forever; and the bread also which I will give for the life of the world is My flesh." [John 6:51]

"but whoever drinks of the water that I will give him shall never thirst; but the water that I will give him will become in him a well of water springing up to eternal life." [John 4:14] So, what's the meaning?

∆∆∆∆∆ *Focus on the Lift* ∆∆∆∆∆

As we continue to build strength and endurance through our *Titanium Transformation*, the fruits of the Spirit are becoming more evident within our lives and relationships. We are given opportunities to share these spiritual yields with others. Galatians 5:22 shares with us the list of spiritual fruits with which the Father has graced us through the giving of His Son's life and the breath of His Spirit. These fruits are: love, joy, peace, patience, kindness, goodness, faithfulness, gentleness, and self-control. On a piece of paper, write each spiritual fruit down the left side of the page, with about five blank lines between each one. Then, today, try to share each of the fruits with someone else. At the end of the day, reflect and write some brief descriptions under each fruit that you listed. This exercise ties nicely with the earlier exercises on weaving stronger relationships. It's a good idea to repeat this writing – doing – reflecting exercise for five more days, or until the fruits of the spirit are evident in your life.

***

When the bough breaks…do we rise or do we fall…
While living in Cincinnati, we experienced a rather severe wind storm one New Year's Eve. Many trees were uprooted where their root systems and branches had been weakened by the hurricane the previous fall (yes, a hurricane in Ohio!), and also as a result of recent snows and ice storms. Two scriptures came to mind that night, so I studied them by candlelight: Ephesians 4:1-6 and Micah 4:1-5. Pray these verses and feel God's presence.

> *Unity of the Spirit*
> Therefore I, the prisoner of the Lord, implore you to walk in a manner worthy of the calling with which you have been called, with all humility and gentleness, with patience, showing tolerance for one another in love, being diligent to preserve the unity of the Spirit in the bond of peace. There is one body and one Spirit, just as also you were called in one hope of your calling; one Lord, one faith, one baptism, one God and Father of all who is over all and through all and in all (Ephesians 4:1-6)

And, Micah 4:1-5:

> *Peaceful Latter Days*
> And it will come about in the last days That the mountain of the house of the LORD Will be established as the chief of the mountains It will be raised above the hills, And the peoples will stream to it. Many nations will come and say, Come and let us

go up to the mountain of the LORD And to the house of the God of Jacob, That He may teach us about His ways And that we may walk in His paths " For from Zion will go forth the law, Even the word of the LORD from Jerusalem. And He will judge between many peoples And render decisions for mighty, distant nations Then they will hammer their swords into plowshares And their spears into pruning hooks; Nation will not lift up sword against nation, And never again will they train for war. Each of them will sit under his vine And under his fig tree, With no one to make them afraid, For the mouth of the LORD of hosts has spoken. Though all the peoples walk Each in the name of his god, As for us, we will walk In the name of the LORD our God forever and ever. (Micah 4:1-5)

Praying these two passages together, teaches us that the Father has gifted us as members of the Body of Christ, and that, filled with His grace, we are called to use our gifts and journey to make a difference in others' lives all in the name of the Lord. In *U R Titanium*, we are learning more about God's provision and our use of His spiritual gifts while we explore God's guidance for working through change, while honing our relationships along the way.

Been there... done that... got the t-shirt...
When clients hire me to teach about managing change, the first thing I do is begin asking questions about the recent, current, and impending changes they are experiencing and facing. Many of us have undergone those so-called "conversion projects" where entire company or organizational systems, whether technological, process-related, functional, or hierarchical, are to be transformed during an expected time interval (which virtually always ends up taking longer than expected) and then the company hires people like me to help keep morale at a preferred level! Yes, we have t-shirts in our closets that read: "I survived the conversion of [insert year... or years]."

That outside assistance approach may work for mitigating distress during organizational change, but what about changes in our individual lives? Let's revisit the personal mission statement exercise that we completed in Chapter 2. Pray about the changes that you need to plan and implement to live your personal mission.

The gift of unconditional love from our Father… we are called to share that gift with others…

When asked to rank the Ten Commandments and share His insight/thoughts on the most important of the commandments, we read Jesus' response in Luke 10:27:

And he answered, "YOU SHALL LOVE THE LORD YOUR GOD WITH ALL YOUR HEART, AND WITH ALL YOUR SOUL, AND WITH ALL YOUR STRENGTH, AND WITH ALL YOUR MIND; AND YOUR NEIGHBOR AS YOURSELF."

While working on a Sunday school lesson on this scripture, a colleague and I were discussing the need for something like a "checklist" to help each of us remember to live this scripture every day. Here is what came to mind after that discussion and some prayerful research:

The calling: We are called to be disciples for Christ. We are called to keep our eyes on Him as we reach out to those around us who need to see Him more clearly. We are called to allow God's light to shine in, on, through, and beyond us, as we journey throughout the path of life each day, one step at a time. Bottom line: we are called to walk with God today and every day knowing that Christ modeled that behavior for us.

Mission: To live as the best disciples we can be for Christ.

New model: W.A.L.K. the T.A.L.K. (Total Awareness of the Lord's Kingdom)

Meaning in the model: We are called to

<u>W</u>alk
<u>A</u>cross the
<u>L</u>ord's
<u>K</u>ingdom, for <u>W</u>e
<u>A</u>re the
<u>L</u>ord's
<u>K</u>ingdom

Jesus invites us to share in the reality of the Cross. As servant-leaders for the Lord, we need to receive this invitation with open minds, hearts, arms, and souls, to fully recognize the significance of His journey in our own lives. This prayerfully designed W.A.L.K. the T.A.L.K. model will help everyone who embraces it, work toward achieving what, as we are called to do in Micah 6:8 " to do justice, love kindness, and walk humbly with our God." Just saw a Missouri license plate today that read: MIC 6 8. Coincidence? I think not.

Prayerfully recognize the need for all of us to live each day with unconditional love for God and each other, and with the desire to reach out to those who need our help.

The test...
One evening after a long day, I was using my husband's car to run an errand, and since I did not have my favorite CD's with me, I was listening to the local Christian station. Suddenly, a pastor came on the air talking about the "1Corinthians 13 Love Test." It was a fascinating discussion. Since then, I found the source of that message: Reverend Richard J. Fairchild's sermon on "The Love Test."[3] Here is 1Corinthians 13:1-10:

> If I speak with the tongues of men and of angels, but do not have love, I have become a noisy gong or a clanging cymbal. If I have the gift of prophecy, and know all mysteries and all knowledge; and if I have all faith, so as to remove mountains, but do not have love, I am nothing. And if I give all my possessions to feed the poor, and if I surrender my body to be burned, but do not

have love, it profits me nothing. Love is patient, love is kind and is not jealous; love does not brag and is not arrogant, does not act unbecomingly; it does not seek its own, is not provoked, does not take into account a wrong suffered, does not rejoice in unrighteousness, but rejoices with the truth; bears all things, believes all things, hopes all things, endures all things. Love never fails; but if there are gifts of prophecy, they will be done away; if there are tongues, they will cease; if there is knowledge, it will be done away. [1Corinthians 13:1-10]

But now faith, hope, love, abide these three; but the greatest of these is love. [1Corinthians 13:13]

Rev. Richard J. Fairchild says, "There is always more growing to do my friends, more growing in faith and love is the test of just how much growing there is for us to do."

Take the test…
Insert "I", i.e., your name, for the word, "Love," to take the Love Test. How does it make you feel? This exercise is both introspective and enlightening.

Love is patient. Love is kind….. I am patient. I am kind.
I am not envious or boastful, arrogant or rude.
I do not insist on my own way.
I am not irritable or resentful.
I do not rejoice in wrongdoing but rejoice in the truth.
I bear all things
I believe all things.
I hope all things.
I endure all things.

[Source: Rev. Richard J. Fairchild's sermon: "The Love Test"]

Let God's love wash over you.

Ginny W. Frings, Ph.D.

Synergy…

"I long to accomplish a great and noble task, but it is my chief duty to accomplish small tasks as if they were great and noble. The world is moving along, not only by the mighty shoves of its heroes, but also by the aggregate of the tiny pushes of each honest worker."---Helen Keller

Recently, I was listening to Steven Curtis Chapman's song "One Heartbeat at a Time,"[4] where he sings about mothers working to make a difference in the world "one little heartbeat at a time" by caring for – and loving their families, while often wondering if what they do each day really matters in the big scheme of things. Many of us mothers have been there asking that same question. The answer is: Yes! When we help others, we are doing so through the grace of God and His smile fills us and those we are helping. We are all being called to a higher purpose while here on earth.

Life is actually designed to be a No Judgment Zone…

The above italicized phrase causes one to think… yes? From a Biblical perspective, it's true. But, in reality… there's not so much evidence of this truth these days. It saddens me to think of how many people get hurt each day by others' words and actions. Now, let's read Romans 14 where Paul calls us out in the way of "principles of conscience."

"Now accept the one who is weak in faith, *but* not for *the purpose of* passing judgment on his opinions. One person has faith that he may eat all things, but he who is weak eats vegetables *only*. The one who eats is not to regard with contempt the one who does not eat, and the one who does not eat is not to judge the one who eats, for God has accepted him. Who are you to judge the servant of another? To his own master he stands or falls; and he will stand, for the Lord is able to make him stand.

One person regards one day above another, another regards every day *alike*. Each person must be fully convinced in his own mind. He who observes the day, observes it for the Lord, and he who eats, does so for the Lord, for he gives thanks to God; and he who eats not, for the Lord he does not eat, and gives thanks to God. For not one of us lives for himself, and not one dies for himself; for if we live, we live for the Lord, or if we die, we die for the Lord; therefore whether we live or die, we are the Lord's. For to this end Christ died and lived again, that He might be Lord both of the dead and of the living.

But you, why do you judge your brother? Or you again, why do you regard your brother with contempt? For we will all stand before the judgment seat of God. For it is written,

"AS I LIVE, SAYS THE LORD, EVERY KNEE SHALL BOW TO ME, AND EVERY TONGUE SHALL GIVE PRAISE TO GOD."

So then each one of us will give an account of himself to God. Therefore let us not judge one another anymore, but rather determine this—not to put an obstacle or a stumbling block in a brother's way." [Romans 14:1-13]

Paul is spot on with his observations and advice for cleaning up and building up our conscience mind, to see others as sisters and brothers in Christ… not to be judged, bullied, or ridiculed, but rather to be loved, supported, and lifted up.

One Body… many members
Remember, God has gifted each of us. Next, to add meaning to the idea of variations in spiritual gifts, let's read 1Corinthians 12:4-31. Then, we will do a *Focus on the Lift* exercise to further thread together our breadth and depth of these gifts into a tapestry… pretty cool image. Give some time for reflection upon completing the assignment.

"Now there are varieties of gifts, but the same Spirit. And there are varieties of ministries, and the same Lord. There are varieties of effects, but the same God who works all things in all *persons*. But to each one is given the manifestation of the Spirit for the common good. For to one is given the word of wisdom through the Spirit, and to another the word of knowledge according to the same Spirit; to another faith by the same Spirit, and to another gifts of healing by the one Spirit, and to another the effecting of miracles, and to another prophecy, and to another the distinguishing of spirits, to another *various* kinds of tongues, and to another the interpretation of tongues. But one and the same Spirit works all these things, distributing to each one individually just as He wills.

For even as the body is one and *yet* has many members, and all the members of the body, though they are many, are one body, so also is Christ. For by one Spirit we were all baptized into one body, whether Jews or Greeks, whether slaves or free, and we were all made to drink of one Spirit.

For the body is not one member, but many. If the foot says, "Because I am not a hand, I am not *a part* of the body," it is not for this reason any the less *a part* of the body. And if the ear says, "Because I am not an eye, I am not *a part* of the body," it is not for this reason any the less *a part* of the body. If the whole body were an eye, where would the hearing be? If the whole were hearing, where would the sense of smell be? But now God has placed the members, each one of them, in the body, just as He desired. If they were all one member, where would the body be? But now there are many members, but one body. And the eye cannot say to the hand, "I have no need of you"; or again the head to the feet, "I have no need of you." On the contrary, it is much truer that the members of the body which seem to be weaker are necessary; and those *members* of the body which we deem less honorable, on these we bestow more abundant honor, and our less presentable members become much more presentable, whereas our more presentable members have no need *of it*. But God has *so* composed the body, giving more abundant honor to that *member* which lacked, so that there may be no division in the body, but *that* the members may have the same care for one another. And if one member suffers, all the members suffer with it; if *one* member is honored, all the members rejoice with it.

Now you are Christ's body, and individually members of it. And God has appointed in the church, first apostles, second prophets, third teachers, then miracles, then gifts of healings, helps, administrations, *various* kinds of tongues. All are not apostles, are they? All are not prophets, are they? All are not teachers, are they? All are not *workers of miracles*, are they? All do not have gifts of healings, do they? All do not speak with tongues, do they? All do not interpret, do they? But earnestly desire the greater gifts.

And I show you a still more excellent way." [1Corinthians12:4-31]

∆∆∆∆∆ *Focus on the Lift* ∆∆∆∆∆

One Body… many members…
One day, I was driving home after teaching a class at the university. The journey home brings me down a street where as one approaches the traffic light at the base of the hill, a beautiful view of the Ohio River and Kentucky on the opposite riverbank comes into view. That day, while approaching this particular intersection, I saw that the cars were lined up waiting for the light to turn green. So, of course I stopped at the back of the line, and while waiting, began noticing the beauty of the snow falling against the backdrop of the river, and then I began to think about how scientists tell us that every snow flake is different, yet they all come from the same sky… insightful moment… caused me to think about how people are all different, but we all come from the same God. We have different gifts and strengths, but God has a purpose for each and every one of us… what are we going to do with the opportunities that God gives us?

For this exercise, you will need a piece of white paper, a pen, and a pair of scissors. Fold the piece of paper in half, and then fold it half, again, and then fold it again (three folds). Use the scissors to cut shapes in the folded paper. When you finish cutting, unfold the paper to see your new snowflake. Next, use the pen to write five words that best describe your personality and what you believe to be your spiritual gifts. Then, for a few moments, reflect on what you have written and ask God to show you ways to share your gifts with others who need you in their lives.

***

Capstone is God's grace…
Recall in Chapter 7, where we completed an exercise directed at recognizing grace within each life. Now, let's read Romans 12 with insights on dedicated service where we are being called to serve one another, and with that comes strengthening of relationships and team building.

"For through the grace given to me I say to everyone among you not to think more highly of himself than he ought to think; but to think so as to have sound judgment, as God has allotted to each a measure of faith. For just as we have many members in one body and all the members do not have the same function, so we, who are many, are one body in Christ, and individually members one of another. Since we have gifts that differ according to the grace given to us, each of us is to exercise them accordingly: if prophecy, according to the proportion of his faith; if service, in his serving; or he who teaches, in his teaching; or he who exhorts, in his exhortation; he who gives, with liberality; he who leads, with diligence; he who shows mercy, with cheerfulness.

Let love be without hypocrisy Abhor what is evil; cling to what is good. Be devoted to one another in brotherly love; give preference to one another in honor; not lagging behind in diligence, fervent in spirit, serving the Lord; rejoicing in hope, persevering in tribulation, devoted to prayer, contributing to the needs of the saints, practicing hospitality. Bless those who persecute you; bless and do not curse. Rejoice with those who rejoice, and weep with those who weep. Be of the same mind toward one another; do not be haughty in mind, but associate with the lowly Do not be wise in your own estimation. Never pay back evil for evil to anyone Respect what is right in the sight of all men. If possible, so far as it depends on you, be at peace with all men. Never take your own revenge, beloved, but leave room for the wrath of God, for it is written, VENGEANCE IS MINE, I WILL REPAY," says the Lord. "BUT IF YOUR ENEMY IS HUNGRY, FEED HIM, AND IF HE IS THIRSTY, GIVE HIM A DRINK; FOR IN SO DOING YOU WILL HEAP BURNING COALS ON HIS HEAD." Do not be overcome by evil, but overcome evil with good." [Romans 12:3-21]

ΔΔΔΔΔ *Focus on the Lift* ΔΔΔΔΔ

The Cross...
Remember that in Chapter 2, we drew a picture of the Cross and then laid our concerns and challenges at the foot of the Cross in our picture. Let's bring out that drawing and prayerfully review the picture and the words. Ok, now that we have been working to spiritually and mentally build through our own *Titanium Transformation*, write down any new perspectives on, or resolutions for, the situations laying at the foot of the Cross. Then, continue to lift them up in prayer. God's grace is covering you… and shining through you as you reflect evidence of His presence.

***

Look at the meaning and purpose shared in Psalm 139…

Psalm 139:1-18…

> O LORD, You have searched me and known me.
> You know when I sit down and when I rise up;
>   You understand my thought from afar.
> You scrutinize my path and my lying down,
>   And are intimately acquainted with all my ways.
> Even before there is a word on my tongue,
>   Behold, O LORD, You know it all.
> You have enclosed me behind and before,

    And laid Your hand upon me.
Such knowledge is too wonderful for me;
    It is too high, I cannot attain to it.
Where can I go from Your Spirit?
    Or where can I flee from Your presence?
If I ascend to heaven, You are there;
    If I make my bed in Sheol, behold, You are there.
If I take the wings of the dawn,
    If I dwell in the remotest part of the sea,
Even there Your hand will lead me,
    And Your right hand will lay hold of me.
If I say, "Surely the darkness will overwhelm me,
    And the light around me will be night,"
Even the darkness is not dark to You,
    And the night is as bright as the day
    Darkness and light are alike to You.
For You formed my inward parts;
    You wove me in my mother's womb.
I will give thanks to You, for I am fearfully and wonderfully made;
    Wonderful are Your works,
    And my soul knows it very well.
My frame was not hidden from You,
    When I was made in secret,
    And skillfully wrought in the depths of the earth;
Your eyes have seen my unformed substance;
    And in Your book were all written
    The days that were ordained for me,
    When as yet there was not one of them.
How precious also are Your thoughts to me, O God!
    How vast is the sum of them!
If I should count them, they would outnumber the sand
    When I awake, I am still with You. [Psalm 139:1-18]

ΔΔΔΔΔ   *Focus on the Lift*   ΔΔΔΔΔ

In this exercise, let's speak Psalm 139 into our lives. What I mean by this idea is to: 1) Recognize that God made you for a purpose; 2) Reflect on His omnipresence in your life; and 3) Respond to His messages that are entering your daily walk to become more aware of His grace in your life.

***

Time to reflect…

As you have been experiencing *Focus on the Lift* exercises in each chapter of *U R Titanium,* you are emerging with more awareness of God's presence and healing in your life. And, throughout this book, you have learned more about yours and others roles as "members of one body – the body of Christ" and how God continues to guide us in the development and use of our gifts to help each other and glorify Him. God calls us to be instruments and messengers – how do we recognize His ringtone and answer His call? Even when the winds of life are blowing at hurricane velocity… I have been there both literally and figuratively. The physical power and communication lines may be down, but God never has interruption in His service to us. He is always there for us. Are we always there for Him, ready and willing to carry out His will for our lives? How do we recognize His voice… calling? I recommend reading my first book, *Navigate with God,*[5] to learn more about the presence of *Golden Moments.* You will build your own Beach House of Resolution and become more aware of the cornerstones of God's presence in our lives.

A menu of opportunity… an aside…
An insight just occurred to me as I was washing dishes after a nice Cajun-themed dinner party we hosted. The dinner guests enjoyed the food and fellowship. I love to cook and find the aromas and spices of Cajun recipes to be tantalizing. When the menu comes together and the house is filled with the atmosphere of culinary creation, I like to

imagine how the dishes will complement each other. I am filled with anticipation as we complete the final "To Do" list before the guests arrive. Our family loves to entertain and break bread with friends… we all have particulars of the preparation for the meal that we enjoy doing… and we work together. For example, I love to cook, but do not like to chop the ingredients – my daughter likes to chop, so we spend time together in the kitchen completing the tasks. This experience causes me to contemplate on the significance of us all being members of the Body of Christ. God has us here on earth to "complement" (with an "e" and not an "i") and work together to further His love and awareness of His presence.

As an aspiring gourmet chef, I enjoy working with new spice combinations when I cook for family and friends. Recently, we had the opportunity to host a Mediterranean dinner party as a company fund - raiser. Every time I cook Greek lemon custard soup – which is becoming a tradition of our Mediterranean dinner parties, I enjoy the nuances of aroma changes as each of the twenty-eight spices is added to the soup cream base…exhilarating sensory experience. And, the dinner guests enjoyed the meal! Question: How do we experience each moment and understand the meaning that God intends for us to see for our lives and relationships? Answer: One spice… one person… one partner… one prayer…one opportunity… at a time. Then, we will see the synergy explode and change lives.

Take-Away

"Finally, brethren, whatever is true, whatever is honorable, whatever is right, whatever is pure, whatever is lovely, whatever is of good repute, if there is any excellence and if anything worthy of praise, dwell on these things." [Philippians 4:8]

Throughout the pages of this book, we have been working together to bring you to realize your own *Titanium Transformation* into a better, stronger, more resilient you. We began the journey prayerfully examining the idea of Trust – why and with whom we need to build meaningful relationships based on trust, and we completed *Focus on the Lift* exercises to sharpen our senses and discernment over whom we should invite to speak in to our lives. Next, we identified Incentives for honing relationships, and learned more about the reasons for becoming stronger mentally, physically, and spiritually. We then drew a picture of our own Cross and placed our concerns at the foot of the Cross. This experience freed us to focus on what God is calling us - both in to and out of – to do in this life. He is calling us into our purpose. Then, we examined the element of Time and recognized how God's timing is the basis for our sequence of achievements when we are seeking to build strength, while following His leadings. As we prayed together while composing our Personal Mission Statements, God continued to reveal reasons for and manifestations of His intended purpose for each of us, and methods for strengthening our physical and spiritual relationships. The Trinity – Father, Son, Holy Spirit – are master communicators into our lives. They teach us daily about Their presence and ways in which we can be stronger for ourselves and for others who need us. After that revelation, we studied Ephesians 6 and acknowledged that donning the Armor of God is imperative as we strive for the strength to recognize and overcome spiritual battles. Next, we accepted an Invitation to high tea with the Almighty… with all the planting, sowing, tending, and reaping needed to harvest and fill our Cup of Compassion. Afterward, we sought Understanding for ours and others' journeys, and ways in which we can help mitigate the challenges and travesties brought with "boulder hopping," and how even a high five can alleviate some tension within someone's difficult day. And, finally, as we try to label these life experiences sprinkled with trials and tribulations, we realize that there is not a formula for living, but rather that each step on this *Titanium Transformation* strength building path brings us to the vertex of our Purpose and Meaning. We have learned new ways to lift up and communicate with ourselves and others. This Take-Away epilogue is deep in meaning. Let's take a few moments to relax and ask the Holy Spirit to help us breathe in this message.

Always remember: You are Strong. You are Resilient. You are Special. You are Loved. You have Purpose. You Can Do This. You are Titanium.

Notes

Prologue
1. Jefferson Lab, education.jlab.org.
2. Online SR-71 Blackbird Flight Manual, www.sr-71.org/blackbird/sr-71/
3. Ginny W. Frings, *Navigate with God* (Bloomington, IN: iUniverse, 2008)
4. David Guetta, "I am Titanium" (Album: *Nothing but the Beat*. Hollyood, CA: Virgin-Capitol US, 2011)
5. Nickelback, "If Everyone Cared" (Album: *All the Right Reasons*. New York, NY: Roadrunner Records, 2005)
6. Casting Crowns, "If We Are the Body" (Album: *Casting Crowns*. Nashville, TN: Beach Street Records, 2003)

Chapter 1
1. Ginny W. Frings, Navigate with God (Bloomington, IN: iUniverse, 2008)
2. Child Development: A Cultural Approach by J. Arnett and A. Maynard, 2005
3. Rick Warren, *Purpose Driven Life* (Grand Rapids, MI: Zondervan, 2002)
4. Michael Card, "Joy in the Journey" (Album: *Joy in the Journey*. Brentwood, TN: Sparrow Records, 1994)

Chapter 2
1. Des Knaben Wonderhorn and Greg Scherer, "Brahm's Lullaby" (Germany, 1868)
2. Casting Crowns, "Voice of Truth" (Album: *Casting Crowns*. Nashville, TN: Beach Street Records, 2003)
3. Merriam-Webster Online Dictionary (c 2005 by Merriam-Webster, Incorporated) www.merriam-webster.com
4. Steven Curtis Chapman, "Declaration of Dependence" (Album: *Declaration*. Brentwood, TN: Sparrow Records. 2001)
5. Ibid.

Chapter 3
1. Merriam-Webster Online Dictionary (c 2005 by Merriam-Webster, Incorporated) www.merriam-webster.com
2. Steven Curtis Chapman, "God is God" (Album: *Declaration*. Brentwood, TN: Sparrow Records, 2001)
3. Merriam-Webster Online Dictionary (c 2005 by Merriam-Webster, Incorporated) www.merriam-webster.com
4. Ginny W. Frings, *Navigate with God* (Bloomington, IN: iUniverse, 2008)
5. Beth Moore, *Discovering God's Purpose for Your Life* (Houston, TX: Living Proof Ministries, 2006)
6. Steven Curtis Chapman, "Miracle in the Moment" (Album: *This Moment*. Brentwood, TN: Sparrow Records, 2007)

Chapter 4
1. TobyMac, "Speak Life" (Album: Eye on It. Brentwood, TN: Forefront Records, 2012)
2. Steven Curtis Chapman, "The Change" (Album: *Speechless*. Brentwood, TN: Sparrow Records, 1999)
3. Michael W. Smith, "Rise" (Album: *Wonder*. Brentwood, TN: Reunion Records, 2010)
4. Ginny W. Frings, *Navigate with God* (Bloomington, IN: iUniverse, 2008)
5. Steven Curtis Chapman, "Treasure Island" (Album: *More to This Life*. Brentwood, TN: Sparrow Records, 1989)
6. Michael W. Smith, "Breathe in Me" (Album: *I'll Lead You Home*. Brentwood, TN: Reunion Records, 1995)

Chapter 5
1. Beth Moore, Discovering God's Purpose for Your Life (Houston, TX: Living Proof Ministries, 2006)
2. Ken Blanchard and Phil Hodges, *Lead Like Jesus* (Nashville, TN: W Publishing Group, 2005)
3. Ginny W. Frings, *Navigate with God* (Bloomington, IN: iUniverse, 2008)
4. Ginny W. Frings, *Blue-Eyed Ruse* (Bloomington, IN, iUniverse, 2014)
5. Michael W. Smith, "I'm Waiting for You" (Album: *I'll Lead You Home*. Brentwood, TN: Reunion Records, 1995)
6. Steven Curtis Chapman, "Way Beyond the Blue" (Album: *More to This Life*. Brentwood, TN: Sparrow Records, 1989)

7. Michael W. Smith, "Rise" (Album: *Wonder*. Brentwood, TN: Reunion Records, 2010)

Chapter 6
1. MercyMe, "The First Time" (Album: The Hurt and The Healer. New York, NY: Fair Trade Services and Columbia Records, 2012)
2. Merriam-Webster Online Dictionary (c 2005 by Merriam-Webster, Incorporated) www.merriam-webster.com
3. Ginny W. Frings, *Navigate with God* (Bloomington, IN: iUniverse, 2008)
4. Michael Card, "Come to the Table" (Album: *Known by the Scars*. Brentwood, TN: 1983)
5. Michael W. Smith, "Mighty to Save" (Album: *A New Hallelujah*. Brentwood, TN: Reunion Records, 2008)
6. Michael W. Smith, "A New Hallelujah" (Album: *A New Hallelujah*. Brentwood, TN: Reunion Records, 2008)
7. TobyMac, "Speak Life" (Album: *Eye on It*. Brentwood, TN: Forefront Records, 2012)
8. Merriam-Webster Online Dictionary (c 2005 by Merriam-Webster, Incorporated) www.merriam-webster.com
9. Beaulah V. Cornwall, *The Chosen Vessel* (Poem).
10. Steven Curtis Chapman, (Album: *Re-creation*. Brentwood, TN: Sparrow Records, 2011)
11. Steven Curtis Chapman, "Meant to Be" (Album: *Re-creation*. Brentwood, TN: Sparrow Records, 2011)
12. Ginny W. Frings, *Navigate with God* (Bloomington, IN: iUniverse, 2008)

Chapter 7
1. Ginny W. Frings, *Navigate with God* (Bloomington, IN: iUniverse, 2008)

Chapter 8
1. 1 Steven Curtis Chapman, "Do Everything" (Album: *Re-creation*. Brentwood, TN: Sparrow Records, 2011)
2. Ginny W. Frings, *Navigate with God* (Bloomington, IN: iUniverse, 2008)
3. Richard J. Fairchild, "The Love Test," www.rockies.net
4. Steven Curtis Chapman, "One Heartbeat at a Time" (Album: *This Moment*. Brentwood, TN: Sparrow Records, 2007)
5. Ginny W. Frings, *Navigate with God* (Bloomington, IN: iUniverse, 2008)

Made in the USA
Monee, IL
06 March 2024

54583947R00111